Options Trading Crash Course

© **Copyright 2020 - All rights reserved.**

The content contained within this book may not be reproduced, duplicated or transmitted without direct written permission from the author or the publisher.

Under no circumstances will any blame or legal responsibility be held against the publisher, or author, for any damages, reparation, or monetary loss due to the information contained within this book. Either directly or indirectly.

Legal Notice:

This book is copyright protected. This book is only for personal use. You cannot amend, distribute, sell, use, quote or paraphrase any part, or the content within this book, without the consent of the author or publisher.

Disclaimer Notice:

Please note the information contained within this document is for educational and entertainment purposes only. All effort has been executed to present accurate, up to date, and reliable, complete information. No warranties of any kind are declared or implied. Readers acknowledge that the author is not engaging in the rendering of legal, financial, medical or professional advice. The content within this book has been derived from various sources. Please consult a licensed professional before attempting any techniques outlined in this book.

By reading this document, the reader agrees that under no circumstances is the author responsible for any losses, direct or indirect, which are incurred as a result of the use of information contained within this document, including, but not limited to, — errors, omissions, or inaccuracies.

to Mary

Options Trading Crash Course

The Best Strategies for Passive Income in 2020. Quick Start Guide for Beginners. Ten Ultimate Profit Secrets.

by Frank Graham Hill

"Don't blindly follow someone, follow market and try to hear what it is telling you."

Jaymin Shah

Table of Contents

Table of Contents 9

Introduction 17

Understanding Options Trading 23

What is Options Trading? 24

Brief History of Options Trading 27
    Thales and the Olive Harvest 27
    Ban on Options Trading activities 29

Why consider Options Trading? 30

Where to Trade Options 32

Advantages of Option Trading 33
    Cost Efficiency 35
    Less risky 36
    Higher profitability 39
    Strategic Alternatives 40
    The bottom line 41

What about the disadvantages 41

Type of Options Trading 43
    Call Option 44
    Put Options 45
    Summary of Call and Put Options 47

Comparison between Options and Stocks 48
    Duration 51
    Ownership 51
    Volume 52
    Market exchanges 52
    Don't Despair 53

Managing Options 57
Positions... 57
   Long Position.. 58
   Short Positions.. 59
      Other Short Positions..................................... 62
   Understanding Synthetic Positions....................... 63
      Why use synthetic position during trading?....... 64
      Types of Synthetic Positions 68

Understanding Options Pricing 77
   Component of Option Pricing 78
      Intrinsic Value... 79
      Examples of Intrinsic Value............................. 80
      Time Value (Extrinsic Value) 81
   Factors affecting Option Trade 83
      Volatility.. 84
      Time of Expiration 87
      Price of Underlying Asset................................ 88
      Options Price (Premium) 89
      Dividend and Interest Rate 89
      Summary of Factors affecting Options Pricing ... 91
   Option Pricing Models 92
      Risk-Neutral Probability................................. 93
      Black-Scholes Model 94
      Binomial Option Pricing Model 97

Treating Option Trading as a Business 103
   Cost of Running Options Trading as a business ...105
   Steps to Starting Trading Options as a Business..107
   Do you have an Options Trading Business Plan?..110

Business Sample Plan for Options Trading 112
What are your goals? 113
Using Your Options Trading Plan 114

10 Ultimate Profit Secret Strategies 119
Secret Strategy #1 - The Married Put 121
Secret Strategy #2 - Collar Call Strategy 124
Secret Strategy #3 - The Straddle Strategy 127
Secret Strategy #4 - The Strangle Strategy 130
Secret Strategy #5 – Call Ratio Backspread 133
Secret Strategy #6 – Long Put Butterfly 136
Secret Strategy #7 – The Iron Condor 139
Secret Strategy #8 – Bear Put Spread 142
Secret Strategy #9 – Covered Call 144
Secret Strategy #10 – Long Put Strategy 146

The Concept of Moneyness 151
Out of the Money 152
At the Money Options 155
In the Money 157
Near the Money 160
Importance of the Concept of Options Moneyness
.... 160

Strategies for Making the Best out of Bad Situations
.... 165
Bad Situation #1 - Misunderstanding Leverage ... 167

- Bad Situation #2 - Undefined Exit Plan 168
- Bad Situation #3 - Trading Illiquid Options 171
- Bad Situation #4 - Legging into spread trades 174
- Bad situation #5 - Trying to recover your loss by doubling up your investment 176
- Bad Situation #6 – Neglecting Upcoming Events . 178
- Bad Situation #7 – Overlooking Index Options.... 180
- Bad situation #8 – using the out of the money call options 182
- Bad Situation #9 – Wasting a longer time before using the buyback short strategies 184
- Keep Learning 186

Managing Risk Effectively in Options Trading 191
- First Group – Probability of Profit over Probability of Loss 192
- Second Group – Amount loss over amount gained 194
- Risk and Money Management 195
- Risk Management Techniques 196
- Why use risk management?.............................. 197
- Nine Effective Risk Management Strategy........... 203
- Ways of Managing Risk 211
  - Risk management using Options Spreads 211
  - Managing risk by diversifying 213
  - Managing risk through options orders 214
- Type of Immediate Risk Management 215

Delta 215
Gamma 217
Theta 219
Vega 221

Money Management and Position Sizing *223*
Improving your money management strategy .. 224
How to determine position sizing 228
How to use position sizing to grow your options trading account 229
Build your trading strategy 230
Identify your best setups 231
Develop your second best setup 231
Determine your maximum daily loss 232
Think in terms of "percentages" 232
Don't be rigid 233

Conclusion 237

Glossary 243

13

"You never know what kind of setup market will present to you, your objective should be to find opportunity where risk reward ratio is best."
Jaymin Shah

Introduction

The concept of Options Trading has been in existence for centuries. Ancient Phoenicians, Greeks, and Romans used options trading based on outbound cargos moving from local seaports.

Nevertheless, when you use the term as a financial instrument, it is an agreement between two parties, which involves a buyer and a seller.

Furthermore, the buyer has the authority but not responsible for selling or buying the principal asset at a predetermined price.

Virtually everyone is scared of investing in the stock market, and it is hard to avoid Options Trading since it is an integral aspect of the stock market.

Most people have considered trading in the stock market a complex process, which requires a quick solution to make big bucks. For others, you have to wear your lucky charm, or else you will join the group of those losing money.

Many people are vigilant when it had to do with investing in the stock market due to the loss many have experience around them.

Apparently, these people did not know that those who lost money are not conversant with the particular stock they are buying. Additionally, these people have no idea of controlling their risks while leveraging their position.

Nevertheless, at the end of this book, you will learn the fundamentals of Options Trading, risks, and the ultimate profit secret strategies of Options Trading. What you get in Options Trading is options contract.

Moreover, within the period of that contract, you either have the option of buying, selling, holding, or handing over options. The control of these assets gives you multiple choices, which could lead to additional profits. This is the primary reason why many clever investors decide to invest in Options Trading instead of buying stock.

With a good introduction, you are ready for a wonderful experience in the world of Options Trading. Do not forget to check the terms page before starting this book, as it will give you the upper edge when discussing important strategies.

Finally, do not practice options trading in a real environment if you are not convinced of your skill. Success happens when preparation and opportunity meet.

When it comes to the financial world, options trading are very different as it is an asset through which value is derived.

In this book, I will expound on options trading, managing options positions, risk management, money management, and important strategies for making the best out of any bad situation. Before going further, it is important to understand the history of options trading in order to appreciate how it has evolved over time. Without further ado, let us begin!

"Confidence is not "I will profit on this trade." Confidence is "I will be fine if I don't profit from this trade."

Yvan Byeajee

Chapter One

Understanding Options Trading

If you have any prior knowledge of the stock market, you meant have heard of options.

Because of its versatility, they are the most common investment you will find in the stock market.

Besides its versatility, options give investors the ability to control their position in the event of the market moving against them.

What is Options Trading?

In this book, I will not assume you know anything about Options Trading. I will try my best to explain everything in a layman term. For beginners, an option is an agreement, which gives the buyer the right to either sell or buy the underlying security or stock at a predetermined price with an expiry date. Alternatively, an option, which operates like a bond or stock, is a security investment.

This means that you (the buyer) predetermine the price of the stock you decide to buy irrespective of the changes, which takes place in the course of the contract period. Normally, one option contract is equivalent to 100 stock of a company. The interesting aspect of options trading is the fact that it binds the seller and buyer into signing a contract that has severe properties with terms to minimize the risk of loss.

For instance, someone wants to buy Alibaba's stock on the NYSE with the current place pegged at $150 per share. After various investigations, you decided that the stock is doing perfectly well with a high chance of its price going higher and decides to use a call option.

The word "call option" may sound strange, but do not worry, I will expound on it later. Just know that in an options trading, there are two options available – call option and put option.

Therefore, with the call options, you have the right to buy Alibaba's stocks at $150. Assuming you bought 15 stocks at $150 per stock precisely 30 days from now. With that contract in your hand, you want about doing other things. Then, 25 days later, you saw an increase in the price, which now hits $250 per share.

Nevertheless, because of the option contract you have to purchase 15 shares of Alibaba's stocks at $150 per share, you can get it at a bargain.

On the other hand, let us assume the price of the stock instead of rising falls down to $100. In this situation, your options contract signifies a loss, and there is no way you want to buy the stocks at $150 if the current price stood at $250 per share. In this situation, you have to allow the options contract to expire before buying the stock at $250 per share.

Boom! That is it. The truth is you didn't see it in that light, or you did not know about it. Perhaps, you can consider the time you wanted to buy insurance for your car. This is similar to when you are doing options trading.

When you buy your car from a dealer, it usually comes with insurance to ensure you in the event of an accident. If an accident occurs, at that time, you do not have an idea of the cost to repair your car, neither are you aware of the current price of the car.

Of course, the price can increase; however, the insurance will help protect you in this situation. Now you understand because Options Trading works exactly like this.

Options Trading give you the opportunity to buy a stock at an already predetermined price. Peradventure, the price does not go the way you anticipated; you have the advantage of allowing the contract to expire while buying the stock later.

Brief History of Options Trading

Hardly can anyone talk about Options Trading without going back in time. Options trading are not a new concept or new form of investment as many people think.

Historians believed that the concept of option trading was first established in Ancient Greece before it was introduced during the formation of the Chicago Board of Options Exchange (CBOE). I will not go deep into history but the basic evolution of Options Trading.

Thales and the Olive Harvest

The first book to have been written with examples of options was in far back 14th century by Aristotle. The book, which was titled "Politics," had an account where the Thales of Miletus made profits from his olive harvest.

Thales because of his interest in various subjects, including mathematics and astronomy, went forward to create the first options contracts.

His study of the stars gave him the ability to predict when the olive harvest season will come.

Because of lack of funds, he wasn't able to buy all the olive presses. Instead, he decided to pay the owners of olive presses some sum of money to have the right to use them during harvest.

As Thales predicted during the harvest period, there was a huge harvest. He sold his rights back to the owners and made some substantial profit.

However, some terms used today weren't used it then, but he created the first call option using the olive presses as his underlying asset or security.

 Actually, Thales paid for the right of the olive presses. However, he lacks the obligation to use the presses at a predetermined price (strike).

Ban on Options Trading activities

Over the years, we have seen the ban on options trading activities in certain parts of the world. This has cut across various countries, including Japan, America, and largely in Europe. However, the most prominent is that of the ban in London, England.

In spite of the growth of options trading, the oppositions weren't overcome; this made trading options illegal until the 19th century.

Today, the story has changed with online trading as popular as ever before. This was attributed to the use of various financial instruments throughout the world.

We have also seen an increased number of online brokers making online options trading more prominent with a large number of amateur and professional traders.

Options Trading are growing rapidly, and I haven't seen any sign of it slowing down.

Why consider Options Trading?

According to Warrant Buffet, "Never rely on a single source of income." This gives you the idea of why you should consider Options Trading because it enables you to diversify your investment while improving your general investment portfolio.

This may come as a surprise to you, but most big corporations throughout the world use options trading as a hedging tactic to defend themselves against losing money when there is a heavy fluctuation of stock prices.

To cut the story short, with Options Trading, you have the advantage when trading and the opportunity to have a larger payout if you decide on selling the stock. The most interesting aspect is the risk management (I will talk about this later).

Just know that as a new investor, you have nothing to worry about your portfolio going bad because it can only get better with Options Trading.

The primary motive behind most people venturing into Options Trading is to make money.

There are various reasons to support their quest because Options trading offers numerous advantages when compared to other financial instruments. However, options trading may not be suitable for everyone, but if you are ready, you can make good money.

The following are some reason why many consider options trading as another source of income.

- Risk management: When you trigger the put options, it offers you the opportunity to hedge against a likely fall in the share value you are holding.

- Speculation: The flexibility of trading inside and outside of options positions affords you the chance of trading options without any intention of putting them to action.

If you anticipate a rise in the market, you may choose to buy the call options. However, you can also trigger the put options if you expect the price to fall.

- Time to decide: When you trigger the call option, you lock the share to the buying price. This gives the buyer adequate time to decide if to exercise the call option and purchase the shares.

- Leverage: This gives you the control to collect high returns from a smaller initial amount instead of investing directly. Nevertheless, leverage comes with its own risk when compared to direct investment.

In general, trading options gives you the opportunity to benefit from a price change without paying the full share price.

Where to Trade Options

This question is a crucial one in the mind of many beginners, looking forward to trading options. While it is quite easy to trade options on various options exchanges in the world, you still need the services of a reliable broker because you cannot make your own transaction.

There are various options brokers to select, and they come in different types. One of the key decisions facing most beginners is their inability to find the best broker to use for their Options Trading.

Advantages of Option Trading

Although options trading began a long term ago, it has a huge reputation as a risky investment that only experts can understand.

However, for individual investors, options trading can be useful in various aspects. In this section, I will expound on the key advantages options offered and how valuable it is adding it to your portfolio.

Recently, options trading have received wide recognition, while many investors try to stay away from it because they believe it is sophisticated and hard to understand.

Others, who have given it a try, have had a bad experience because of their poor background in trading. This situation has led to major problems with many discouraging others from taking part in trading.

Furthermore, terms like "dangerous" or "risky" have been attached incorrectly to options trading by various financial media and public figures in the financial market.

Notwithstanding, it is vital for investors not to conclude based on this bad experience without getting the other side of the story. This will be impartial and inappropriate to conclude that options trading is risky and dangerous suddenly.

In this book, you will understand four key advantages you will benefit as an investor trading options. With these advantages, you will understand why many people have considered it risky and dangerous.

Cost Efficiency

Trading options gives you great leverage. Because of this, an investor can get an option position that is similar to a stock position but which offers better cost-saving opportunity. For instance, you buy 100 shares of a $40 stock, which must result in a payout of $4,000. Nevertheless, if the investor decides to buy two $10 calls (remember each contract is equivalent to 100 shares), the total cost will be $2,000 (2 contracts x 100 shares x $10). The $10 is the market price. From this, the investor has an additional $2,000 to use for whatever purpose.

Although it is not as easy as you see it because the investor must select the right call to buy to make such profit.

For clarity, let us use another example. Assuming you want to buy Apple's share because you anticipate it will rise within several months. So, you bought 150 shares of Apple while it is trading at $120; the total cost would be $18,000.

Rather than spending so much more, you would decide to select the option imitating the stock closely and purchase the August call option with a predetermined price of $60, for $16. To get a position as the same as the 150 shares aforementioned, you have to buy two contracts. This will bring your investment to $32,000 (2 contracts x 100 shares x 16 current market price), which opposes the $18,000 you could have invested.

Less risky

In Options Trading, you will find situations where buying the options is riskier than you owning equities. Nevertheless, sometimes, you will find when options can help you reduce your risk.

However, this depends on how you choose to use them. Options trading are less risky for traders because they don't require much financial commitment when compared to equities.

Options are safer than stocks because they are the most reliable aspect of hedging. If an investor buys stock, he has to place a stop-loss order regularly to protect this position.

The purpose of putting the stop order is to stop losses when it reaches its predetermined price set by the investor. In as much as this looks good, the issue is that it depends on the nature of the order.

For instance, you decide to buy a stock at $150 but don't want to lose anything below 15% of your investment.

So you decide to place a stop order at $145. This order will be activated once the order sells at or below $145. Peradventure, you woke up the next morning after seeing the stock closed at $151 the previous day and heard that the CEO of the company wasn't truthful concerning the earning reports.

Furthermore, there were rumors of embezzlement in the company with the expectation that the stock will open around $120. Once this happens, $120 will be your first trade below the stop order you placed at

$145. Immediately, the stock opens, it will first sell at $120. The stop-loss order you activated wasn't there to "save" your investment when you need it.

Peradventure, you trigger the put option to protect your investment, it couldn't have affected you. Options are different in the sense that they don't shut down even when the market closes.

They provide insurance every day of the week. Stop orders cannot do this for you. This is the reason why options are a more reliable aspect of hedging.

Additionally, instead of buying the stock, you could have used the stock replacement strategy, which allows you to buy an in the money call option rather than buying the stock.

With certain stock options, you can mimic an equivalent of 75% of the stock performance; however, this cost one-quarter of the stock price.

If you had bought the $145 predetermined price call rather than the stock, your loss would have been limited to the amount you spent. If the option cost you only $6, your loss would have been only $6 rather than the $31.

Higher profitability

There is no need to use a calculator to find out if you are making the same profit as you are losing money because options trading come with higher returns.

The example below will clarify that.

Using our previous example, we will make a comprehension of the percentage returns when you bought the stock at $50 and $6 respectively.

Let's assume the option has a delta of 70. This means the price of the option will change 70% of the stock's price change.

Peradventure, the stock rose to $5; the position of your stock would return a 10% increase.

Strategic Alternatives

The last benefit to Options trading is the alternative investment opportunity it offers. Options Trading offer a flexible tool and allow investors to recreate their options in many ways.

These positions are called synthetics and offer investors with different means of achieving the same investment goals for their trading.

Despite the fact that synthetic positions are regarded as advanced in options trading, they offer various strategic alternatives for investors.

For instance, most investors use brokers who charge a margin when the investor decides to short a stock. However, some investor doesn't use brokers that offer a margin.

Using options in your trading as an investor allows you to trade the "three dimensions" of the market if you like.

The bottom line

From the advantages below, you can agree that those who say Options trading is risky and dangerous are only one-sided.

Frankly speaking, the opportunity in options trading is limitless, especially if you undertake to time to understand every aspect of option.

Options trading signify the dawn of a new era for anyone looking to diversify their business or investment. Don't be left behind when you can be at the forefront.

What about the disadvantages

You may be thinking, are there any disadvantages to options trading? Well, anyone who tells you no is only deceiving you.

Options trading is a short-term investment, and there are bound to be some disadvantages. For instance, if you mistakenly make a wrong prediction on a particular trade, within the next couple of months, you will lose money instead of waiting for years.

Another disadvantage is taxes. You think because you trade online, you won't pay tax. You got that wrong because everything you do on the Options trading market require you paying tax.

However, in certain rare cases, you may not pay. Therefore, include that in our business plan and ensure to fill your IRA form before you start investing.

Additionally, you won't have any certificate of deposit when you trade options, unlike shares. The only thing you get when trading options is your paid rights, and this doesn't prove ownership of the option.

Besides this, the issue of uncertainty is a turnoff for most investors. It is scary to invest in something you have no knowledge about. Because of this, most investors take the time to understand everything about the market and investing. With that knowledge, they can easily turn a loss into a profit. The important thing is to know the strategy you want to use. Endeavor to start small; take only trade you can afford to lose. Options' trading is like learning how to drive.

At first, everything looks scary and impossible. However, with time behind the wheel, you begin to perfect your driving skills. Over time, you start using a single hand to turn the steering; options trading works in a similar fashion. To be at the top, you have to practice, learn, and unlearn what you have learned.

Type of Options Trading

Remember the call and put options? Yah let us expound on them before going further.

Get this at the back of your mind that a buyer triggers the call option, whereas the seller triggers the sell option.

Call Option

A call option gives the buyer the right to purchase the underlying shares at a preset rate, on or before the predetermined date. Nevertheless, the buyer, at this point, expects the price to rise.

But, this is tricky, and you need to be cautious because if you buy the stock at an increased price and decides to go along with it, you may end up losing all your investment.

Remember, once you buy the stock, there is no limit to the amount of loss you can make. Once your loss increases, the losses keep on increases.

The market can be volatile at times, which means at one moment you may have everything and in a snap lose everything.

Once you put the call option into actions, you have the following rights to:

- Buy a specific quantity of the asset

- Buy at a specific date

- Buy at a specified price

    Those who buy options are called holders

Put Options

The slight difference of the put option to the call option is the fact that the holder has the right to sell the stock or asset at a predetermined price in the future.

The put option is similar to when you have a "short on a stock."

This means you expect the price of the stock to fall, and once that happens before the contract expiration period, you make a profit.

You can use this strategy to your advantage, especially when you know the price will fall after a period.

However, it is important to note that the price may never fall but instead rise before the expiration of the contract.

This should not discourage you because the best part of a put option is once the price falls, you are certain to earn high profit. Alternatively, if things did not go as you expect, you will not lose your money.

If you want a quick profit without investing in the asset for a longer time, then you may consider taking the put option strategy.

Most experienced investors' looks for opportunities when the asset price falls before they make a move. When the price falls, it places them in an advantageous position to reap the market.

Those who sell options are called writers

Summary of Call and Put Options

The call options give the buyer (holder) the right to buy the asset from the seller (writer) at a predetermined price (exercise price or strike) within a specific period of time before expiration.

Those who buy the call option are bullish whereas the sellers of calls are bearish.

Alternatively, the put option gives the buyer (holder) the right to sell the asset to the seller (writer) at a predetermined price (strike) within a specific period of time before its expiration.

The buyers in this situation (put option) are bearish, whereas the sellers are bullish.

Comparison between Options and Stocks

I have indicated in this book that options is a contract, and the holder (buyer) has the right to buy or sell the underlying asset at a predetermined price pending the end of the contract. Most times, the stock is the underlying asset of the option.

However, this doesn't mean there are no other assets to trade on. You can also use other assets such as foreign currencies, commodities, stock indices, exchange-traded funds, and government currencies.

Generally, a stock option is equal to 100 shares of the stock of a particular company. An options contract constitutes the following things:

- An underlying asset
- A predetermined price
- A number of shares
- An expiration date
- An option type – call or put

Most time, many investors prefer to trade stock options because of their high leverage and limited risk. An investor only loses the total price for the options contract.

When trading options, the buyer loses the premium price he paid for whereas, in stock options, the seller predetermines the price of the stock for a period. An investor stands to profit more using leverage in options trading that stock.

For instance, John who is an investor, bought 100 shares of FPC stock at $100, which amounts to a cost of $10,000. Aside from the stock, John also has 5 $100 premium call options with a predetermined price of $100 per share.

This allows him to buy 500 shares. Perhaps, recent news made the price of the share to increase to $110 after a month; this would amount to a profit of $1,000.

Assuming the option premium for the stock rise from $100 to $300, what will be the outcome? For John's normal stock investment, he will get a 10% profit, whereas the value of his stock option will be a 50% profit.

However, if he decides to activate his five options by buying an additional 500 shares at the rate of $50,000 while selling it later at $55,000, his net profit will be $5,000.

This example looks profitable because the leverage favors John. What happens when the price goes in the wrong direction? His percentage loss will be magnified.

That is the downside of using leverage in options trading. From the example above, assuming the share price took a dip to $80, John's will experience a loss of 20%.

Alternatively, his option premium will decrease to $80, thereby resulting in an overall 60% loss.

This is why many investors are cautious when using leverage in options trading. If you can predict the markets properly before you invest, it will be a huge bonus to you.

Duration

Another comparison to check between options trading and stock is the time frame for the trade.

Generally, stocks don't have an expiry date. This means that the stockholder can choose to hold the stocks indefinitely.

However, an option is different as it has a predetermined expiry date. The option becomes valueless when you don't exercise it before the expiry date.

Ownership

To own a stock share, you must have a certificate from the company stating your ownership of the share. However, options do not require any certificate of ownership.

It is simply an agreement, which holds the option. Options do not require any papers.

Volume

Another distinguishing feature of stock and option is that you are issued a certain number of shares.

Investors have a limited number of shares to trade, which is normally 100 shares for each stock option. Nevertheless, there isn't any limitation as to the number of stocks you can buy or sell as an investor.

Market exchanges

Institutions, individual investors, and professional traders trade options through an options exchange. There is every possibility for an investor to transact various options contracts concurrently. Just as the regular stocks, you can trade the stock option but on a regulated market by SEC.

Don't Despair

Most brokers will discourage you from venturing into options trading. Their primary reasons being that the propensity of losing money is high.

However, this does not hold true as with adequate knowledge concerning the underlying asset and your ability to manage risk effectively; you can reap big profits.

Meanwhile, it is important to state that the lack of knowledge when trading is equivalent to losing money before starting. Options Trading is like any kind of investment.

To succeed, you have to learn the strategies, scenarios, and other things to stay ahead of the market and have a long smile at the end.

Although this may seem like a boring adventure, once you pass through the initial learning period, you will be motivated to know more.

Don't forget to start small. Move slowly as it will help you build a strong foundation that will put your ahead.

"The expectation that you bring with you in trading is often the greatest obstacle you will encounter."

Yvan Byeajee

Chapter Two

Managing Options Positions

In options trading, the investor can take two different positions – a short or long position. The investor can sell an asset (going short) or buy it (going long).

Ordinarily, you will think that is all but this position is further complicated by the two types of options – the put and call option (check chapter One).

What this means is that the investor can take four different positions – a short call, a short put, a long call, and a long put. Additionally, experienced investors can combine short and long positions to form complex trading and hedging strategies.

Long Position

During a long position, which is also a buy position, the investor is anticipating a rise in the price of the stock. Such a rise in the stock price will be profitable for the investor.

A long call position is a situation where the investor buys a call option. Therefore, a long call position is also beneficial if the price of the stock rises.

The basic concept behind the long aspect is the same as that of a long call. The value of a put option rises when the option or asset drops in value.

In terms of the long position profits, the potential loss in a long asset purchase is the purchase price of the option. However, the upside is limitless.

Moreover, for the long calls and puts, the profit downsides are complicated.

Short Positions

The second position in Options Trading is the short positions. It is the opposite of the long position explained. The investor anticipates a decrease in the price of the option to gain profit. Executing a short position is not as easy as when you buy an asset.

Using a short stock position as an example, the investor expects profit if the price of the stock drops. This is possible by borrowing a number of shares from a stakeholder of a particular company while selling it at the current price.

With this, the investor has an open position for the number of shares he or she bought with the broken. Remember, this stock has a particular timeframe before it will be closed.

Peradventure, the price of the stock drops, the investor has the right to buy the number of stock shares lower than the total price he sold them previously.

The excess cash for this trade is the profit of the investor.

Most investors find it hard to understand the idea behind short selling; however, it shouldn't be complicated. Well, to clarify this, the example below can make things clear for you. If after this you do not understand, then Options Trading is not for you.

ssuming the stock of NCE is currently sold for $50 per share. For some reasons, you anticipate a fall in the price of the stock and decide to sell short in order to make gain from your anticipation. How then should your short sale look like?

- You place a margin deposit as collateral to your broker to give you a loan of 100 stock shares

- With the loaned shares given to you, you sell it at the price of $50 per share. With this, the share isn't yours anymore; however, in your account, you have $5,000 ($50 x 100 = $5000). In this situation, you are short of stock because you are in debt of 100 shares to your broker.

- Assuming your expectation that the price would fall happens gradually. After some weeks, the price dropped to $30 per share. Furthermore, you expect the price not to go any lower, so you decide its time to close the sale.

- You then bought the 100 shares at the price of $30 amounting to $3,000. You decide to repay the 100 shares of stock you borrowed from your broker.

- With the 100 stocks, you were able to make a profit of $2,000 by activating a short trade. When your broker loaned you the shares, you received $5,000 ($50 x 100 =$5000) and after buying you were able to pay back your loan amounting to $3,000. Amount received ($5,000) − Amount Paid ($3,000) = Profit ($2,000)

Short positions are usually given to accredited investors because it requires a high level of trust between the broker and the investor in order to execute this deal. Actually, it doesn't matter if the short is executed; the investor must place collateral that the broker will use in exchange for the loan you want to take.

Other Short Positions

A short call position is activated when an investor sells a call option. The position is the opposite of the long call. The seller is in a better position to profit short call position is activated, and the value of the asset or stock drops.

Alternatively, when the investor triggers a put option, the seller profits if the value of the option traded is higher when compared to the predetermined option price.

Options trading come with varieties of long and short positions for you to adopt during trading. A knowledgeable investor who understands the advantage and disadvantage of all individual position will always be ahead of the market.

However, if you are a new trader, don't rush to apply for these positions. Understand each position before making an effort to combine into your trading strategy.

Understanding Synthetic Positions

A synthetic position is a trading position formed to imitate the features of another position. The concept behind creating a synthetic position is to recreate the same reward and risk profile of another trade. In options trading, there are two ways of creating synthetic positions.

Firstly, you can do that through a combination of the different options contract to imitate a short or long position of the stock.

Secondly, you can also combine it with stocks and options contract to imitate a trading strategy. Generally, a trader can create six different synthetic positions for various reasons.

The concept of synthetic positions may sound confusing for some traders. Some may even wonder the need for creating another position from a preexisting position.

However, the truth about synthetic positions in options trading is that they are not essential. There is actually no reason to use them.

In spite of this, they have certain benefits when applied during trading. In this section, I will explain why most traders use synthetic position before providing details on the six different synthetic positions.

Why use synthetic position during trading?

Options traders use synthetic positions for a number of reasons with most primarily revolving on the flexibility and cost efficiency they offer when used. Although some reasons are uniquely attached to the different synthetic position, essentially, there are three main benefits and these are closely related.

Firstly, synthetic positions are flexible, meaning that you can change from one position into another when your prospect changes.

With this, you don't need to close your current position. For instance, you have written a call in anticipation that the price of the underlying stock will drop within the upcoming weeks.

However, because of an unforeseen change in the market environments, you believe the stock price will increase.

If you want to benefit from the increase in price like the one you would have done when your anticipation was a drop in price, then you will have to close the short position with a possible loss while writing a put option.

Nevertheless, you can recreate your options previous short position by buying an equivalent amount of the underlying stock.

The benefit of using the synthetic position in this situation is that you only have to place a single order to purchase the stock instead of placing two different orders to close your short call position. Furthermore, you have to open the new short put position.

The second benefit of using a synthetic position is similar to the previous one. once you hold a synthetic position, you can easily benefit if the position moves towards your expectation.

Don't worry; the example below will make it clearer for you. Assuming you made a short put on an option, expecting a rise in the stock for a small amount.

In this situation, the best you will get is the amount received for selling the contracts. It doesn't matter if the price goes up or not.

Perhaps, you held a short put position and anticipated an increase in the price of the stock; however, your outlook on the stock position changes and you believed the rise in the stock would be quite significant, and then you have to enter a new position in order to maximize your profit.

Then you have to buy back the put option you wrote and either buys call on the stock. Nevertheless, if the synthetic position you held in the first position is short put, then you can close the short call position while holding the stock to profit from the anticipated rise.

The third benefit of using a synthetic position is due to the flexibility it has. Flexibility means you make less transaction.

Changing from an existing synthetic position into another synthetic position because of the change of your expectation requires fewer transactions when compared to pulling off from an existing position to enter another one.

Types of Synthetic Positions

Synthetic Long Stock Position

This is a position where a trader to emulate a potential outcome of actually owning a stock using options.

To create this position, a trader will have to buy at the money calls on the stock before writing at the money put on the same stock.

The money you got for selling puts will recoup the price paid for this calls.

This means that if your stock fails to move in terms of price, you will either gain or lose anything.

The benefit of using this position is the leverage involved.

Your initial capital required to create this position is lower than buying the corresponding stock.

Synthetic Short Stock

This is similar to selling short stock but used on options only. Creating a synthetic short stock requires selling at the money calls on the stock and later buying at the money puts on the same stock.

There are two benefits of using this position when trading. The first deals with leverage, while the other is related to dividends.

Synthetic Long Call

This position is created why a trader buys a put option and buys the underlying stock.

The combination of using put options and owning stocks on the underlying stock is as effectively comparable to owning a call option.

You can apply for a synthetic long call position if you own put options and anticipate a fall in the price of the underlying stock.

However, if your anticipation was wrong and the stock price increase, instead of selling your put options before buying the call options, you can decide to recreate the payoff characteristic by purchasing the stock while creating a synthetic long call position.

This is helpful, as it will reduce your transaction cost.

Synthetic short call

This position is created why you buy put options and buy the underlying stock. The combination of put options and acquiring the stock based on the stock is equivalent to owning call options.

Synthetic Short Call

This position involves an investor writing a put and short selling the stock.

Combining these two positions will effectively recreate the feature of a short call option.

A synthetic short call position is used when your trade is short on puts with the expectation that the stock price will rise.

However, you believed that the stock would fall; instead of closing the short put options and then entering a short call, you can recreate your position to allow place a short call.

The benefit of this is that it reduces your transaction costs.

Synthetic Short Put

This position is useful when you anticipate an increase in the price of the underlying stock by a moderate amount.

The short put position comes to effect when you have been previously anticipating a contrary event to occur.

Assuming you held a short call position and decides to switch to a short put position, and then you have to close your current position while writing a new put.

Nevertheless, you can create a synthetic short put rather than buying the stock.

Combining the stock you own with the short call position, you can have the same profit and loss.

Synthetic Long Put

This position is the last type of synthetic positions in options trading. You can use it when you anticipate a rise in the underlying stock.

However, if after some time, your expectation changes to a fall in price, a synthetic long put position can save the day.

If previously you place call options expecting a rise, you can short sell the stock.

Combining long and short calls on the stock is almost the same as holding a put option on the stock.

If you have created a call option, creating a long put position will require you to sell those calls while buying the puts. However, holding on the calls while shorting your stock, you make fewer transactions, thereby saving you more cost.

*"Losses are necessary, as long as
they are associated with a technique
to help you learn from them"*
David Sikhosana

Chapter Three

Understanding Options Pricing

For instance, a particular company sells its shares for $50. After researching, you find the company worth investing, and the price look nice. Actually, the price is what triggers your thought.

Instead of buying the shares out rightly, you agree to increase your prospective gains by procuring some call options. Assuming your anticipation comes out successful, the price will increase along with the value of the options. However, instead of this, you are confronted with certain questions like, which options to invest in? What price to buy? What is the expiry date?

In case the stock price increases, how will the options price react? What will happen if the price goes against you? What happens once the expiration date gets closer?

Component of Option Pricing

There is basically two component of an option price, which includes intrinsic value and the time value. The option price is a summation of these two components.

Therefore, the addition of intrinsic value and the time value gives you the equivalent option price.

Option Price (Premium) = Intrinsic value + time value

Are you confused by these terms?

If you still do not understand option pricing, don't worry because most investors at the initial stage experienced the same thing. To make it easier, option pricing is similar to an insurance premium.

Intrinsic Value

The intrinsic value is the difference between the stock price and the predetermined price.

Nevertheless, *the intrinsic value can never be lower than zero*, since the buyer won't trigger the call option with a predetermined price of $50 if the current stock is trading at $30 in the market. (If you find someone that would do this, please don't hesitate to contact us.)

Perhaps you might have heard of the terms "out-of-the-money" and "in-the-money," well, don't confuse yourself.

You consider an option to be out-of-the-money if there is no intrinsic value for it, whereas in-the-money occurs when the value is greater than zero.

There is another scenario, which is at-the-money, which takes place when the intrinsic value is equivalent to zero. I will explain more in the concept of moneyness.

Nevertheless, the calculation for the intrinsic value is different for the call and put options.

For the call option, the intrinsic value is the market stock price minus the predetermined price, whereas for the put option; it is the predetermined price minus the market stock price.

Call option (intrinsic value = market stock price – predetermined price)

Put option (Intrinsic value = predetermined price – market stock price)

Examples of Intrinsic Value

For instance, the stock of Honeywell Limited (HL) is selling at $36.90. The HL 32 call option would return an intrinsic value of $4.9. This means that the buyer triggers the call option to buy HL shares at $32 while turning around later to sell it at $36.90, which is a profit of $4.9. Remember the call option is the market stock price minus the predetermined price ($36.90 - $32 = $4.9)

Time Value (Extrinsic Value)

The time value or time premium is a representation of the amount someone is willing to pay in anticipation that the market will favor him or her within the period of the option.

Another name for time value is extrinsic value because of the potential value it adds to the option based on the movement of the stock in the future. The time value is determined by subtracting the intrinsic value from the option price.

Time value = Option price – intrinsic value

In time value, the longer the expiration period, the greater the option time value. The figure below shows that.

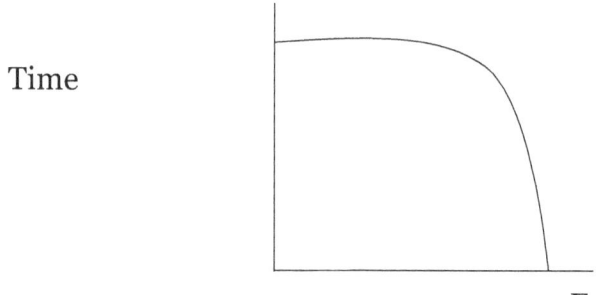

From the example above, if HL stock trades at $36.90 with a month expiration and HL call option of $32 are trading at $8, the time value of the option is $4.9. Remember time value is option value minus intrinsic value ($8 - $4.90 = $4.90).

However, if the stock of HL trades at $36.90, with a call option of $32 at $6 with a 9-month expiration period, the time value will be $2.90. ($6 - $4.90 = $2.90).

Factors affecting Option Trade

It is hard to know where you are going unless you have been there before. It is impossible to price an option unless you know what makes up the value.

Options trading can become a sophisticated machine of legs, adjustments, multiple orders, and Greeks. Nevertheless, without the fundamental, you will be running in circles.

Have you ever thought about how options prices come about? Amazingly, these prices are not randomly generated instead calculated using various models. Later, I will talk about the various Options Trading Models as it relates to Options Pricing.

Before attempting to venture into options trading, you must understand the basic factors responsible for affecting an option price.

Nonetheless, having a good understanding of the science behind option pricing will help you harness trading and meet your investment goals. Various factors are responsible for the price of an option.

These factors include the stock price, volatility, intrinsic value, time value, cash dividend paid, market expectation, and interest rates.

Some of these factors have more significance, while others have lesser significance during trading and require sophisticated mathematical models to calculate.

Volatility

Volatility is a major factor in option pricing that plays a major role in strategy selection and options analysis. In the stock market, those that are stable have lower option prices when compared to those with extreme volatility. The effect of volatility on the option price is harder for any beginner to assimilate.

Besides this, there is also implied volatility, which is founded on the market marker belief. If the number of persons investing in a particular stock increases, the tendency of the price increase is high. However, the market marker can control the implied volatility to upturn the option price.

An option trading as a versatile investment serves as a better and cheaper substitute for stocks. It offers better profits via leverage while limited your overall risk.

What this means is that you won't be putting all your eggs in one basket, hoping it doesn't go against you. Additionally, an option is valid pending the expiry date; therefore, nothing like your money getting tied down forever.

However, you can only lose money to the amount of your option price, which is the amount you paid for at the initial situation. Alternatively, the seller must either buy or sell the asset peradventure the buyer activates his option.

Importantly, the seller has the right to amount paid by the buyer; however, this takes effect if the buyer fails to either sell or buy the underlying asset before the expiration of the contract.

Volatility can be tricky at times. It can be profitable if you are in a favorable position. However, if you are on the opposite side, you can lose something substantial.

Due to the impact volatility has on the option price; it is advisable to trigger the buy option when the market is quiet while selling during the period of high volatility.

Investors who prefer to hold long options when there is a high explosion in volatility tends to enjoy notable profits. Alternatively, short option traders might be in a less anticipated position if they experience a major increase in volatility after entering their position.

With an increase in volatility, both the call and put options increases in terms of value. The reason behind the value increase of the call option is due to the increase in the underlying price because of high volatility.

Correspondingly, the underlying price may fall if there is a lower price because of the high volatility.

Time of Expiration

Options come with time value and the more time pending the expiry of the option, the higher the time value, and the option price.

Every option must have a fixed expiry date.

The option price keeps decreasing every day, no matter the changes in the price of the underlying assets.

Beginners in Options Trader find it hard to understand the importance of the time of expiration of a trade.

Subsequently, they suffer from losses mistakenly.

However, Options writers take advantage of the time of expiration.

Once the expiration time gets closer, the option value begins to decrease.

Price of Underlying Asset

This factor is crucial in options pricing because everything is based on it. The price of the underlying asset determines both the call and put options, along with you want to invest in.

The call and put options move in different directions – when the price of the asset increases, the call option increases.

Nevertheless, if the asset price increases, the put option prices decrease. This shows that change in the price of the asset in the market affects the option price directly.

Alternatively, when the price of the asset decreases, the call option decreases while the put option price increases.

Most investors will trigger a put option if the asset is important for a short time.

However, a call option is exercised in the case of an asset with potential. Importantly, the longer the expiry time, the greater the option price of the asset.

Options Price (Premium)

The option price for an option displays a different reaction to the fluctuations in the market price of the underlying asset.

Changes in the price of an Options price favor the predetermined price, which is closer to the current price of the asset

Dividend and Interest Rate

Although this factor doesn't have much significance for trading purposes; however, they show the interest rate earned on the cost of carrying the dividend yield and trade value.

A high-interest rate will lead to higher option prices.

The reason behind this is that high-interest rates compete for the money of an investor when compared to low-interest rates.

Investors will rather control the price of an asset of an option price when interest rates are high than buying it outrightly.

If the interest rates are high, it makes investors choose options instead of assets.

Therefore, the interest rate drives the option price.

Summary of Factors affecting Options Pricing

Factors	Call Option	Put Options
Volatility	Directly proportional	Directly proportional
Time of expiration	Directly proportional	Directly proportional but with exception to long-dated options
Price of the underlying asset	Directly proportional	Inversely proportional
Option Price	Inversely proportional	Directly proportional
Dividend & Interest rate	Directly proportional	Inversely proportional

Option Pricing Models

Option Pricing models are simply mathematical models, which uses certain variables to estimate the theoretical price of an option.

The theoretical price is an estimation of what an option is worth after using every recognizable input.

Understanding option pricing is crucial because it gives you a fair value of an option.

If you want to trade options like a professional, then you have to equip yourself with this knowledge.

In this section, we will explore a few pricing models to enable you to figure out the price of an option.

Fundamental knowledge of these models will put you ahead.

Nevertheless, let us cover some of the basic models in the Options Trading world.

Risk-Neutral Probability

Before going into the different Option pricing models, it is important to understand risk-neutral probability because you will come across it when we start discussing the price models.

Risk-neutral probability is a speculative possibility of future results regulated for risk. The concept of risk-neutral probability has two main assumptions, which are:

- The current asset value equates to the anticipated payout reduced during the risk-free rate

- The market doesn't have any arbitrate opportunities

The idea behind this concept is that there is a chance that the price of the stock would increase in the risk-neutral world. With that sorted out, we can dive into the pricing models.

Black-Scholes Model

It is one of the famous pricing models used in Options Trading.

Two economists, Fischer Black, and Myron Scholes, discovered the model in 1973 and were given the Nobel Memorial Prize in economics for their innovation.

This model was designed to be used for the pricing of European Options for stocks and works under certain hypothesis about the economic environment and stock price distribution.

The hypothesis for the stock price distribution includes:

- Unremittingly accumulated returns on the stock are usually spread and autonomous over time.

- The unremittingly accumulated returns are recognized and constant

- Future shares are known

The hypothesis regarding the economic environment includes:

- The risk-free rate is unchangeable and known

- There are no taxes or transaction costs

- There is the possibility to short-sell without any cost and also to borrow without any risk rate

However, these two hypotheses don't apply to a certain situation.

In addition, this model can be used to price options on assets apart from stocks. Furthermore, the main variables of the Black-Scholes Model include:

- The current price of the underlying asset

- Implied volatility

- Predetermined price (strike)

- Time until expiration

- Risk-free interest rate

- Dividend rate

The Black-Scholes mathematical formula might look complex for a beginner. An average investor may find it hard to use the formula.

However, you don't have to stress yourself over it because there are various options calculators available online to calculate option price using this model.

Additionally, different trading platforms provide analysis tools to enable investors to calculate the option price.

The Black-Scholes pricing model is an efficient means of getting an estimate of your investment.

Nonetheless, it is advisable not to depend on it because of the sudden changes, liquidity risks, and the volatility nature of the market.

The model can expose you to major risks that may affect your investment. You can use the model to get a glimpse of the option price, but it is important for you not to rely on it completely.

Binomial Option Pricing Model

Unlike the Black-Scholes Pricing Model, the Binomial model is much simpler to understand and apply. It uses the hypothesis of perfectly effective markets. In this hypothesis, the model has the capability of pricing the option at a certain point under a definite timeframe.

The assumption under the Binomial Option Pricing model is that the price of the asset may go either down or up within that timeframe.

Putting the likely price of the asset and its predetermined price, one can calculate the payoff of the option based on these scenarios. Later, the payoff is discounted, and you find the current value of the option as it stands today.

The hypothesis of the Binomial Option Pricing Model

The assumptions of the model are as follows:

- It is based on an effective market
- Only two prices exist for the future
- The two prices are known on downtick or uptick
- There is no possibility of an arbitrage

- The interest rate remains unaffected during the period under contemplation
- No transaction cost exist

"When you learn to let go of the need to be right, being wrong gradually lose its power to disturb you."

Yvan Byeajee

Chapter Four

Treating Option Trading as a Business

Have you ever thought about all the occupations in the world? Have you considered the time and investment people put in? The owners trusted you to perform such a job.

If you are one of the owners, will you allow anyone to perform their duty without any knowledge or training? Of course, you will not think about that.

Even if you decide to do a menial job that does not require any higher education, you will still need some sort of training. As menial as a dishwashing job may be, it has its techniques, the same way it is when you want to perform a surgery. Both jobs are very differen, but they do require you to follow instruction.

In the same manner, a person who finds a website and starts trading options in the market without any prior knowledge and instruction may succeed but for a while. However, "this career" will be short-lived, as his funds will disappear suddenly.

On second thought, won't it be better to take your time and learn everything required to be a good trader? The result is always impressive, but the process requires dedication.

Well, trading is very different from other occupations or business, although it is still a business. Running your Options Trading as a business will go a long way rather than just desiring to make huge money and improve your lifestyle.

Most traders start on the wrong foot, and I want to avail you this opportunity to start on the right path.

You must recognize that Options Trading is not like taking a trip to one of the prominent casinos in Las Vegas. Treating Options Trading as a business requires planning and structure.

It also involves a cost to get the business running successfully. To begin as a successful options trader, you must run and view Options Trading as a full-term business.

Cost of Running Options Trading as a business

Similar to any kind of business, the easiest means of making a profit is by generating more profits than your costs. Undoubtedly, you will agree to this statement because if you continue to lose money, you will ultimately reap off your business.

All professional traders will tell you never to allow your cost or capital to become larger than your revenue or profit.

For options trading, the primary cost of running it as a business is losing trades. Does that sound right? Well, it should if you want to be a successful trader. At the back of your mind, always consider losing trade as your cost of trading options.

It is important to see them that way and never allow your emotions to becloud or influence your judgment. At times, you must think like a restaurant owner, who does not get unhappy or angry because customers made a re-order of their food.

Any trader who told you he or she hasn't lost trade in their entire career is simply lying to your face. Every successful trader on Earth, irrespective of how profitable they may be, might have lost a trade once in their career.

So when you begin your journey, you shouldn't be perturbed by the temporary losses. They are unavoidable, but you can always beat the market.

Furthermore, you must be prepared to deal with them at all cost

Steps to Starting Trading Options as a Business

Interestingly, stock options trading offer great opportunity to reap profits because you can control about 100 shares for each stock option with your risk limited to the option price. There are no much trading instruments, which can offer such leverage with limited risk.

However, upcoming option traders find it hard to make a profit, because they lack the skill to trade options like any business. Well, if you follow the steps below, then you are sure on the right path to trading options like any professional. So how do you begin your options trading as a business?

First, you need to find a professional options broker in the market. Today, we have numerous brokers (both real and fake) looking for beginners like you to make an investment.

However, you have to be diligent in searching the internet and conducting interviews where applicable. If you know anyone who has been in the market, you can ask for a recommendation.

If you decide to take the first route, then you must ask the broker how long they have been trading options. Ask them their take on the difference between Ratio Backspread and Calendar Spread.

The truth remains that working with an experienced broker is a valuable asset, especially in a volatile market like the Options market.

Secondly, choose a reliable trading platform, which incorporates your brokerage account, price charts, and offer the buy/sell features openly with your broker. Successful businesses take time and adequate planning to succeed; this you must be willing to do if you want to thrive in options trading.

Ensure you perform a background check on the various trading platform, read reviews of their previous clients to ascertain if they are the right choice. You will not want your business to hit the ground before you begin.

Thirdly, once you are convinced of the platform, you can then open your Options trading account. Different brokerages have their minimum amount you can use to open an account.

Some offer as little as $1000; however, averagely, most brokerage accepts $5000 in order to open an account. Nevertheless, these always come with certain limitation to your account.

Fourthly, you should set up two different screens – one to track your underlying stock after setting up the price charts and the second for the stock symbols. Additionally, you need another separate screen to view the option quotes of the stock you are tracking.

Do you have an Options Trading Business Plan?

Perhaps you have heard that. However, what is the requirement for anyone to succeed in this market?

Top traders, along with investors, will always place discipline as the key to success.

That is the truth because without discipline, you will allow a losing trade develop into a portfolio murderer.

Two essential ingredients if you want to succeed in options trading are education and knowledge.

However, your efforts and money will be in total vain if you lack the discipline in following a prearranged trading plan.

For some, trading options come with frustrating challenges, while others get a lifetime financial reward. Where you fall among these two groups, depends on you.

Writing a solid trading plan is essential, as it will expose your trading approach, risk, and money management tactics.

A sound training plan will highlight the kind of trades to take, those to avoid, your risk control, and trade management. After gathering all knowledge, you need to spend a large chunk of your time on your trading plan. Do you want to treat Options Trading as a business?

You cannot run away from having a practical business plan for your business. It is the bedrock of you building a successful option-trading career.

Fact: Most upcoming option traders start to fail when they neglect to have a comprehensive trading plan. For others who start but fail to complete all the necessary plans, at the end regret it.

Timing your trade and control your risk is too important to be neglected in your trading plan if you want to trade profitably and operate Options Trading as a business.

Business Sample Plan for Options Trading

This business plan will integrate different aspects of trading you may be familiar with if you are a professional. However, if you are a beginner and new to the trading environment, then it will be more beneficial.

As already stated, trading options is similar to any kind of business. It is not enough to think that trading is a business, but you must put into consideration every detail that has the capacity of influencing your success and affecting your overall cost-effectiveness. There are specific costs that need to be covered if you want to take it as a full-term business.

Perhaps, you will need computer costs, tax implications, price data fees, and fees for using the trading platform. Your electricity bills aren't exempted from it because it has an impact on your profit.

Options trading plan is a documentation of everything you require to operate your trading business smoothly. It includes your money management, trading strategy, what to trade, and the valuation process of trades. Before you consider creating your trading plan, you need to define your objectives or goals.

What are your goals?

What do you want to achieve in this newfound business? What are your personal developments, financial, or trading goals?

Financial goals

- As a yardstick, what profit are you expecting per month or year?

- Are you going to use different strategies when faced with different market situations?

Personal development goals

- How will you improve yourself?

- What will you do if your financial goals aren't met?

- What will be your reaction to drawdown periods?

Using Your Options Trading Plan

When you have a comprehensive trading plan, it shows strategies and restrictions for your trading activities. Practical use of your trading plan is to enable you to manage your risk exposure and money. Because of this, it is important to include information on the capital to use and the level of risk that won't affect you.

Once you follow your plan and use your money judiciously, you will not be a victim of the biggest mistakes traders and investors make. With this, you won't use scared money as the case of most investors.

If you decide to trade with money you can't afford to lose or meant for another purpose, you will make rational decisions while trading. Although it is hard to take emotion during Options Trading, it will pay you better to remain focus on the primary motive of your trading.

Once emotion sets in, you start losing your focus and begin to make illogical decisions. For instance, this could lead to you chasing losses from previous trades, which has gone wrong.

However, if you have a plan, follow it, and stick to use your investment capital, you stand a better possibility of keeping your emotions in check.

Likewise, you must stick to the risk level outlined in your trading plan. If you decide that low-risk trades are your best strategy, there isn't any need for exposing yourself to trades with higher risks.

At times, it is tempting to trade with higher risks after making some loss with the "believe" of fixing them. Most times, this does not turn out as expected. However, you don't have to cage yourself; you should consider stepping out of your comfort, especially when the risk involved isn't high.

"You don't need to be a rocket scientist. Investing is not a game where the guy with the 160 IQ beats the guy with 130 IQ." – Warren Buffett

Chapter Five

10 Ultimate Profit Secret Strategies

Options Trading are an art that involves a process to be successful. Developing definite steps and rules is part of the process to get you moving the right direction towards becoming a skillful trader.

Implementing these processes with a focus on managing risk offers you the time required to build your craft. The first step of that process requires creating your own strategy list.

With this, you can methodically approach different trade in order to acquire the needed knowledge and experience.

My motive in this chapter is to unveil the top 10 profit secret strategies to use when trading options. The strategies mentioned here have limited risks with alternatives to consider. Each strategy will include:

- The strategy name and its components

- The risks involved and rewards

- Maximum market conditions (volatility, trends)

- Merits and demerits

- Basic risk profiles

Many traders and investors have lost huge money trading options without fully understanding the ins and outs of the market. However, having a solid strategy is essential to make a profit when trading. It allows you to maximize your profit while mitigating your risks.

These strategies take a little effort to learn them and use them effectively. Nobody will see an opportunity to maximize their profit and decide not to give it a shot. Will you look the other way round?

Secret Strategy #1 - The Married Put

Investors use this strategy when they are bullish about the price of the asset. It requires investors to buy the asset and concurrently purchase the put options for a corresponding number of shares. The primary motive behind this is to safeguard their asset in case of likely losses on a short-term.

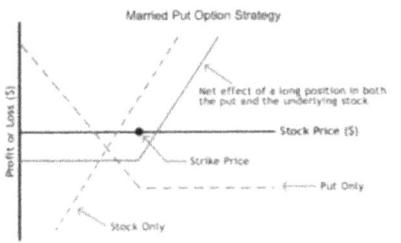

The Married Put strategy is simply a means of taking advantage of an investment at the moment without having to worry about losing it when things get tough.

The prospect for profit when using this strategy is limitless. The strategy is akin to insurance that defines a floor price peradventure the price of the asset experience a dramatic dive. From the graph above, you will observe two different lines – a dashed line with a straight line.

The dashed lines represent the long stock position. From the combination of the long stock position and a long put, it is clear that as the price of the stock falls, the losses are limited.

When to apply the Married Strategy

The perfect opportunity to apply the married strategy is when you anticipate the price of the stock to rise considerably before the expiration of the option. Although, you also consider there is a tendency of the price falling considerably too. This strategy gives you the opportunity to hold the asset or stock while enjoying any potential upside in the market if there is any rise. Additionally, your investment still has coverage if there is any substantial loss peradventure there is a fall.

Summary of the Married Put Strategy

Strategy	Outcome
Reward/Risk	Unlimited Reward/Limited Risk
Component	Long Put + Long Stock
Maximum Reward	Unlimited
Maximum Risk	((Put Price + Stock Price) − Predetermined price)) * 100
Margin	Not normally required
Condition	Bullish
BreakEven	Put Price + Stock Price
Advantage	Limited changes
Disadvantage	Increases the cost of the position

Secret Strategy #2 - Collar Call Strategy

This strategy is a combination of the protective puts, short call, and long stock.

You use the selling call along with the put-call against the stock.

The primary reason investor use this strategy is due to their out of money option.

When to apply this strategy

The collar call strategy is effective, especially when you want to gain premiums option and don't want to risk any potential loss in the future because of a price reduction or security risk.

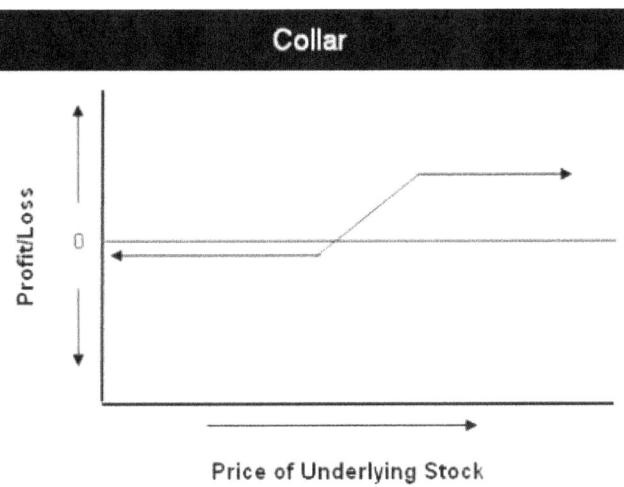

Price of Underlying Stock

It is understandable if you do not understand this strategy because most traders find it hard at the initial stage. Let us put it this way, to create a collar you must first own the commodity.

Furthermore, you have to write an out of the money call option before receiving a premium for doing so. With the premium on the option, you can buy them out of the money put option.

Consequently, if the stock falls, your loss will be limited because of the put option. On the other hand, if the stoke goes up, you can still make a little bit limited profit on that upward trend.

Summary of the Collar Call Strategy

Strategy	Outcome
Reward/Risk	Limited Reward/Limited Risk
Component	Long Put + Long Stock + short call
Maximum Reward	((Call predetermined price - Stock Price) + Option Debit) - 100
Maximum Risk	Stock Price + (Option Debit) – Put Strike Price] -100
Margin	Not normally required
Condition	Bullish
BreakEven	Stock Price + Option Debit
Advantage	Limited changes
Disadvantage	Changes unlimited reward with limited reward

Secret Strategy #3 - The Straddle Strategy

Most option investments require an investor to buy single security, which becomes profitable if the stock moves in a particular direction.

However, rather than expecting a specific direction, you can use the straddle strategy.

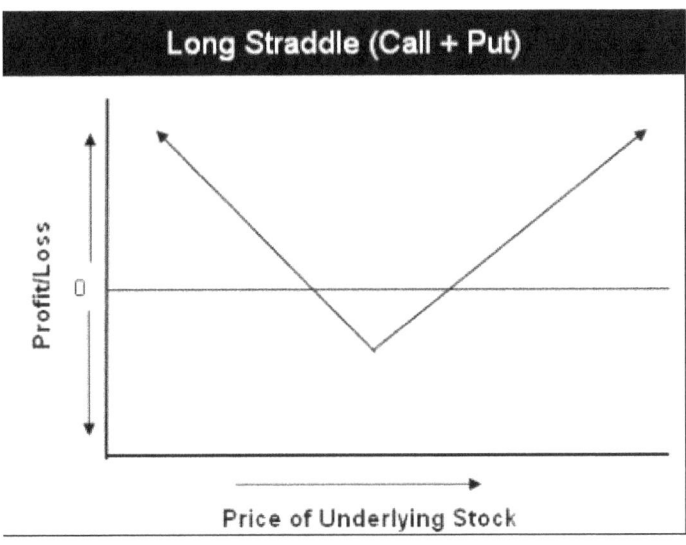

The strategy allows you to buy both a put and call option under the same predetermined price and expiry date.

It doesn't matter the direction the stock moves; it becomes profitable as long as the movement is enough to cover the option price for both contracts.

Summary of the Straddle Strategy

Strategy	Outcome
Reward/Risk	High to unlimited Reward/Limited Risk
Component	Long Put + Long Call (Both at the same predetermined price)

Maximum Reward	(Predetermined Price − Net Debit) × 100
Maximum Risk	Net Debit = (Put Price + Call Price) × 100
Margin	Not normally required
Condition	Bullish
BreakEven 1	Predetermined Price + Net Options Prices
BlackEven 2	Predetermined Price − Net Options Prices
Advantage	Reduces movement risks of a single option positions
Disadvantage	Increases cost of a single option position

Secret Strategy #4 - The Strangle Strategy

At first, the strangle strategy looks like the straddle strategy.

Although they both have features of buying a call and put option with the same expiry date; however, the difference is that they are bought at different predetermined prices.

Investors use this strategy when they anticipate that the stock price will move significantly but does not know the direction of the price.

The best time to enter this kind of strategy is when there is extreme volatility, especially in earning season.

This allows the investor to move into the position at a lower cost because of one or both of the options contracts can be bought out of the money.

This means it won't be valueless buying at the current value of the stock. In as much as this strategy offers a less expensive position to enter, it does also require more movement before it gets more profitable than the straddle strategy.

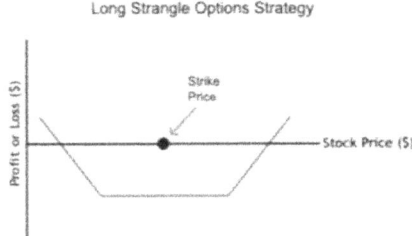

From the diagram above, you will notice two breakeven points. The strangle strategy turns out to be profitable if the stock makes a movement in any direction.

The investor doesn't care the particular direction of the stock, but his major concern is that the move should be a greater move when compared to the option price paid for such structure.

The risk in this strategy is limited to the initial premium paid while the reward is unlimited. Furthermore, the upper breakeven point is gotten by adding the predetermined price of the call option with that of the net premium paid. The lower breakeven point is the difference between the predetermined price and the net premium paid.

Summary of the Strangle Strategy

Strategy	Outcome
Reward/Risk	Unlimited/Limited Risk
Component	Long Put + Long Call (Different predetermined price)
Margin	Not normally required
Condition	Bullish
BreakEven 1	Predetermined Price + Net Options Price
BlackEven 2	Predetermined Price – Net Options Prices

Secret Strategy #5 – Call Ratio Backspread

This strategy is one of the complex strategies to understand in Options Trading. You should only use it if you fully understand the different options of trading instruments.

However, the Call Ratio Backspread is a combination of three or more options positions. It combines a long call with a lower predetermined call expiring at the same moment.

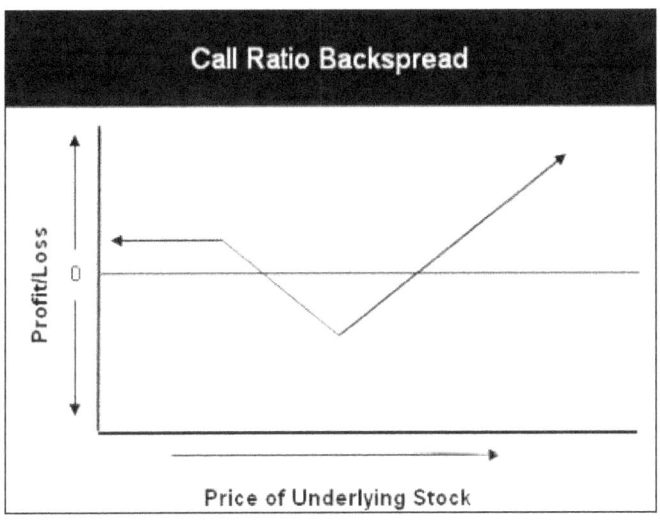

When to apply this strategy

The best time to implement this strategy is when there is limited risk with a highly unlimited reward.

The strategy is also similar to the straddle strategy because investors make a profit when the price of the stock falls.

Using this strategy, you have to buy and sell different call options at a different predetermined price within the same expiry date.

Summary of the Call Ratio Backspread

Strategy	Outcome
Reward/Risk	Unlimited Reward/Limited Risk
Component	Long Call + Lower predetermined price (Expiring at the same month)
Maximum Reward	Unlimited
Maximum Risk	Limited
Margin	Required
Condition	Bullish
Advantage	Limited reward changes to unlimited rewards
Disadvantage	Complex calculation and difficult to understand

Secret Strategy #6 – Long Put Butterfly

The strategy comprises the combination of two different option positions.

If the strategy comes with the call option, the investor will combine the bull spread and bear spread strategy together and use three different predetermined prices.

All options have the same expiry date.

For instance, you can construct a long butterfly spread by buying a single in the money call option when the predetermined price is low while selling two at the money call options and also buying an out of the money call option.

The long call butterfly strategy is similar to the short straddle strategy except for the fact that the losses are limited.

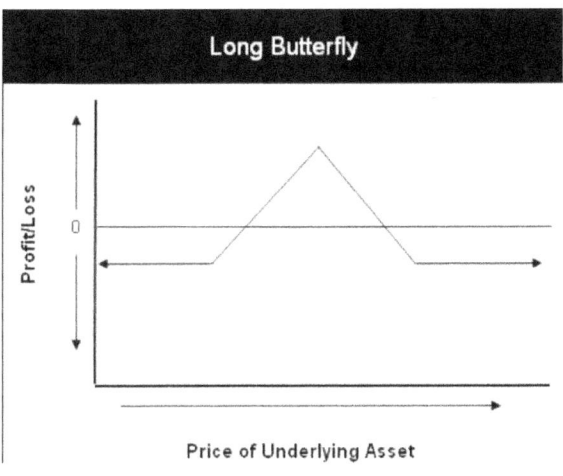

When to apply this strategy

This strategy is implemented by investors when they anticipate little movement or stagnation in the price of the stock.

The investor in this situation is aiming at making a profit at a low cost from a low volatility situation.

Summary of the Long Put Butterfly Strategy

Strategy	Outcome
Reward/Risk	Limited Reward/Limited Risk
Component	Bear Put Spread + Bull Put Spread (same expiration date)
Maximum Reward	[(Highest Predetermined Price – Middle Predetermined Price) × 100] – Net Debit
Maximum Risk	Net Debit: [(Lowest Predetermined Put Price + Highest Predetermined Put Price) – (2 × Middle Predetermined Put Price)] × 100
Margin	Required
Condition	Slightly Bearish
BreakEven 1	Highest Predetermined Price + Net Debit Price
BlackEven 2	Lowest Predetermined Price – Net Debit Price
Advantage	Moves from unlimited to limited risk
Disadvantage	The three positions incur an additional cost

Secret Strategy #7 – The Iron Condor

Unlike the strangle and straddle strategy that is easier to implement, the Iron Condor is very difficult and not the best strategy for beginners to use.

It requires adequate practice and time to perfect. Investors hold a bear call spread with a bull pull spread simultaneously to implement this strategy.

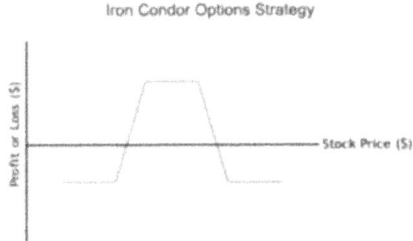

However, it is put together by buying and selling each out of the money put at a lower predetermined price (bull put spread) and selling and buying both a single out of the money call at a higher predetermined price (bear call spread).

The option has the same stock or underlying asset and expiration date.

From the graph above, you will observe that the maximum profit is achieved when the stock rests in a moderately wide trading range. However, the wider the stock moves towards the short predetermined price, the higher the loss

When to apply this strategy

You can implement this strategy when you anticipate that the stock will trade in relatively low volatility pending the expiration of the options.

The good side is that when done correctly, you eventually buy low while selling high. What this means is that you induce profit again.

For beginners, don't confuse the predetermined prices. The outcome is always selling higher and buying lower if you put it correctly.

In terms of risk and reward, the Iron Condor strategy offers both limited risk and reward.

The up breakeven point is equivalent to the highest predetermined price plus the net debit.

The down breakeven point is the lowest predetermined price minus the net debit.

Secret Strategy #8 – Bear Put Spread

This strategy allows investors simultaneously buying at a higher predetermined price while selling at a lower predetermined price on the same asset with the same expiry date.

You can implement this when the market is moderately bearish, and you anticipate a short-term fall on the stock.

However, there is a net premium on the stock because the Put option is bought at a higher predetermined price than the selling Put.

Furthermore, the risk level is limited to the premium paid, whereas the reward is limited.

The breakeven point is gotten by removing the net premium paid from the Long Put predetermined price.

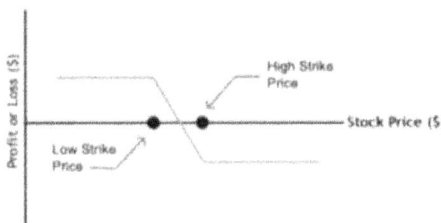

From the graph above, the strategy is bearish because you need the stock fall for you to make a profit.

The interchange when using a bear put spread strategy is that the upside is limited, whereas there is a reduction in the premium spent.

Secret Strategy #9 – Covered Call

The covered call strategy is a common strategy that even new investors understand because it reduces their risk while generating income. The trade-off with the covered call strategy is that you have to sell your shares at a predetermined price. To implement the covered call, you must buy the stock as would have done.

Then instantly trigger a sell call option on the same shares you bought. I will use a call option for this example, which is a representation of 100 shares of stock for each call option. It means that you have to sell a call option for every 100 shares of stock you purchase.

Investors can implement this when the direction of the stock is neutral to bullish.

Interestingly, both the risk and reward are limited. The breakeven point is the price of the stock minus the premium received for the option.

Secret Strategy #10 – Long Put Strategy

In our last secret strategy is the most popular strategy in Options Trading. It is the reverse of buying a Call.

When you buy a put option, you are bearish, whereas for the Call option you are bullish as regard the stock.

The Long Put options furnish the buyer the right to sell the stock at a predetermined price, which further limits his risk.

It allows investors to take advantage of the market when they anticipate it falling. The risk is limited to the premium paid on the stock, but his profits are unlimited.

Bearish investors utilize this strategy when trading stocks or index.

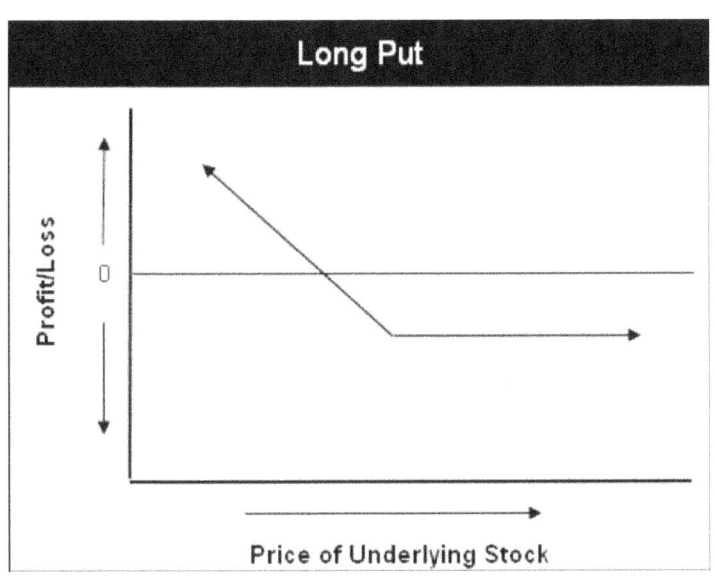

"That cotton trade was almost the deal breaker for me. It was at that point that I said, 'Mr. Stupid, why risk everything on one trade? Why not make your life a pursuit of happiness rather than pain?'"

Paul Tudor Jones

Chapter Six

The Concept of Moneyness

The concept of moneyness is an easy concept to explain in options trading because it isn't complicated.

It is one of the fundamentals of options trading, and you must be conversant with it.

When you hear options traders use the term "moneyness," he or she refers to the relationship that exists between the predetermined price (strike) and the current price of the stock.

In this chapter, I will describe the three main terms used in describing the concept of moneyness in options trading. These terms include in-the-money, at-the-money, and out-of-the-money. There is also a fourth term, near-the-money.

In our previous chapter, I gave a brief explanation of the first three terms; nonetheless, I will expound more with illustrations to make it easier for you.

Finally, you will understand the importance of the concept of moneyness in Options Trading. Let's explain these concepts.

Out of the Money

You consider an option to be "out-of-the-money" in options trading when the option does not have intrinsic value. What this means is that the call option is out-of-the-money when the predetermined price is higher than the stock price.

Meanwhile, a put option will be out-of-the-money if the predetermined price is lower or below the stock price.

Alternatively, out-of-the-money is a situation where the underlying asset or security is trading at a price that does not favor the buyer of the options.

Remember in the first chapter, I indicated that an option price comprises of two components (intrinsic value and time value).

The intrinsic value deals with profits that exist in an option, whereas the time value is influenced by different factors, including expiration time, volatility, interest rate, the value of the underlying asset, and dividend.

Consider the out-of-the-money option for both the call and put options.

Call Options for Out of the Money

Price of Stock	Call Option	Intrinsic Value	Out of the Money
$100	$120	$0	Yes
$140	$80	$60	No
$150	$165	$0	Yes

Put Options for out of the Money

Price of Stock	Put Option	Intrinsic Value	Out of the Money
$100	$120	$20	No
$140	$80	$0	Yes
$150	$165	$15	No

Call option (intrinsic value = market stock price – predetermined price)

Put option (Intrinsic value = predetermined price – market stock price)

Do you remember the formula above in Chapter Three? From the formula, can you understand how come about the various value in the table? Of course, you should.

At the Money Options

You can say an option is "at-the-money" when the predetermined price is equal to the stock price.

Similar to the out-of-the-money concept of moneyness, it does not have intrinsic value.

This concept is applicable to both the call and put options.

Furthermore, this concept is expensive than the previous money option because the price of the stock has to move below in order to create intrinsic value.

Although the definition of the at the money options is when the predetermined price is equivalent to the price of the stock, it is rare to find such a situation since the stock price is ever changing.

Price of Stock	Call/Put Option	At the Money
$100	$140	No
$165	$165	Yes
$160	$170	No

In the Money

This concept is an option with intrinsic value. The call option and put option are both different.

A call option in the money situation occurs when the stock price is higher than the predetermined price, whereas the put option occurs in a situation where the stock price is lower than the predetermined price.

They are the most expensive moneyness concept in options trading.

Additionally, many experts recommend this concept for beginners because it is easier to regulate risks if peradventure they cost more.

Let us assume you own this option, and the expiry date is fast approaching, it is better to sell them because once

it gets to the point of expiration, they are automatically exercised. This may not be what you want to see.

Call option of "in the money."

Price of Stock	Call Option	Intrinsic Value	In the Money
$100	$150	$0	No
$140	$80	$60	Yes
$150	$120	$30	Yes

From the call option above, you can see that when the call option price is below the price of the stock, it means it has intrinsic value.

Put Options of "in the Money"

Price of Stock	Put Option	Intrinsic Value	In the Money
$100	$120	$20	Yes
$140	$80	$0	No
$150	$165	$15	Yes

The table above shows that when the call option price is higher than the stock price, then it is in the money because the put option has intrinsic value.

Near the Money

Although this moneyness concept isn't part of the three aforementioned standards, however, it is used commonly. It occurs when the predetermined price is close to the price of the stock or asset. This moneyness concept is either slightly between the out of the money or in the money options.

Importance of the Concept of Options Moneyness

A fundamental understanding of the concept of options moneyness and its various states is quite simple for anyone to assimilate. They are common phrases used in options trading and are essential for you to be conversant with them.

Irrespective of the options trading strategy you employ, you do require the fundamental knowledge of moneyness state. Perhaps you are using a simple strategy that requires a single position; you still require the concept of option moneyness.

For instance, if you decide to buy a stock and anticipate that the price will move dramatically in a short period, then using the out of the money option will be the best option to maximize your profits. However, if you anticipate a little movement, then in the money option provides a better and less dicey investment.

Immediately you start using complex strategies in options trading; the concept of moneyness becomes important in your trading. Different advanced trading strategies require several positions on different options.

For these strategies to work effectively, it is crucial to trade options using the right moneyness concept. For instance, a particular strategy may require you buying an option and later selling out the option of the same stock.

If you lack the knowledge on the concept of moneyness, you will make the mistake of buying or selling the option in the wrong moneyness state. However, you can navigate through this situation if your knowledge of moneyness is well-polished to use the right trading strategies properly.

Hurry! You have the knowledge of the concept of moneyness. You are not in the dark anymore whenever a trader talks about using moneyness. You can navigate your way through any situation you face in the market.

"The elements of good trading are: (1) cutting losses, (2) cutting losses, and (3) cutting losses. If you can follow these three rules, you may have a chance."

Ed Seykota

Chapter Seven

Strategies for Making the Best out of Bad Situations

Human beings, by nature, are creatures of habit. Habits can make or mar us. They have a great impact on our lives.

Some are dangerous and have every tendency of breaking us apart in life or business.

Options traders are not exempted because the habit they form during their trading beginning can influence almost all of their decisions.

Every professional options trader knows that getting into a bad situation is part of the game. Although, the issue isn't about getting into such a situation but making the best out of such a situation.

Interestingly, most of these bad situations are avoidable in the course of trading. Perhaps, it is possible to see your stock go upward, downward, or sideways.

Irrespective of the situation, you can use the strategies in this book to protect your gains, cut losses, and control your stock using a little cash outlay.

Does that sound great? Well, here is the real deal. There is every possibility of blowing up your entire money invested during trading.

Therefore, you have to take every precaution necessary for such to happen again if you have been there.

If you are new to Options Trading, do not despair because confident traders have misjudged opportunities and lose their investment.

This chapter covers the topmost bad situations you may face as a beginner trading option. It also includes tips to outsmart the situation.

If you are a beginner, don't rush over this section as you will learn what most options trader learned the hard way. Options Trading aren't easy. Don't make it harder than it ought to when you have everything to make things right.

Bad Situation #1 - Misunderstanding Leverage

Many people misuse leverage when trading option. They do this without realizing the amount of risk they are taking.

Most times, they indulge in buying short-term calls. Most beginners are the culprit in misunderstanding the use of leverage in their trading.

How to make the best of this situation

There is no better way of handling this situation than mastering leverage. A general rule, if you are new to Options Trading, is to stick to a particular option when starting.

However, if you trade 100 share lots stay with a single option; however, if you trade 300 share lots, you can trade 3 contracts. After using these different lots and still not successful, don't try to increase the trade size, thinking you will be successful.

Bad Situation #2 - Undefined Exit Plan

Perhaps you have heard this repeatedly to take control of your emotions during trading. It doesn't matter what kind of trading you are involved. However, it does not mean swallowing every fear that comes your way in a heroic way.

Remarkably, it is quite simpler than you imagine. Irrespective of the response, you are getting from your emotions, stick to your plan, and never deviate from it.

How to make the best of this situation

Having an exit plan is not primarily about reducing your loss if things get in a bad situation. Even if the trade is going the way you anticipate, an exit plan isn't an option to ignore. You must put into consideration your downside and upside exit point before trading any option.

It is not enough to have a downside and upside price targets when trading; you should plan the timeframe for every exit you set. Don't forget that the options you trade are a decaying asset. Furthermore, the rate at which these assets decay accelerates fast as your expiry date comes closer.

Therefore, if you traded a long put or call and your prediction doesn't go the way you anticipate within the timeframe, don't wait rather pull out of such trade. You don't have to be a victim of time decay. You can sell options without owning them, and this will make the time decay to work to your advantage.

In summary, you need and must have an exit plan for every trade irrespective of the particular strategy you implement. You don't have to stay long on trades that have gone against you, hoping to move to your favor later. Once you hit your profit, move out of the market.

If you want to establish a successful pattern of trading option, it is advisable to have a plan. In addition, keep your emotions where it belongs. Trading options is exciting, and you shouldn't expect a onetime wonder hit.

Therefore, get your exit plan fixed in advance and stick to it until the day dawn on your trade.

Bad Situation #3 - Trading Illiquid Options

Assuming you have a quote for a particular option, you will observe a difference between the call option and the put option.

Alternatively, some traders refer to the call and put options as the biding and asking price, respectively. The bid price is the amount the buyer is willing to buy the option, whereas the asking price is the price the seller is willing to sell the option.

Oftentimes, the call and put option is not a reflection of the worth of the option. However, the option value lies between the biding and asking price.

Furthermore, the extent to which these prices differ from the option value depends on the liquidity of the option.

When you hear about the liquid in Options Trading, It refers to a situation where there are both active sellers and buyers with high competition to complete all transactions. Liquidity drives the stock and options price closer.

Liquidity in the stock market is different from that of the options market because stock trader's trades only stock whereas those trading options on a particular stock have different options contracts to select from, with each having a different predetermined price and expiration dates. Illiquidity in Options Trading is a major issue, especially when you have to deal with illiquid stocks.

Peradventure the stock is inactive, the options will undoubtedly be far more inactive like the stock whereas the spread between the bid and ask will be wider. All of these may sound strange but assume that you want to trade on an illiquid option, which has a bid and ask price of $2.00 and $2.25 respectively. You will observe there is a 25-cent difference, which may not be big money for you.

Even if you saw it lying on the floor, you won't think of picking it up. However, in Options Trading a 25 cents for a $2.00 option position is a 12.5% rise in price.

How to make the best of this situation

Trading illiquid options increase the cost of doing business.

However, with Options Trading, the cost is already high.

Maybe you are trading options; ensure your open interest doesn't go below 40 times the amount of option contracts you want to trade.

For instance, if you were to trade a 10 share lot, the acceptable liquidity to allow should be 400 (10 x 40).

Open interest shows the number of unsettled options contracts of a predetermined price with an expiry date that hasn't be sold or bought to open a position.

The main idea is to trade liquid options while saving yourself the additional stress and cost.

There are numerous liquid opportunities to take advantage out in the market.

Bad Situation #4 - Legging into spread trades

Legging may sound strange, but it is a situation where at a time you enter the different legs of a multi-leg.

For example, when you trade a long call spread, you may be lured to buy the long call before thinking of selling the short call using an uptick in the price of the stock.

Nevertheless, the market at times becomes downtick, and you cannot remove you any of your spread.

In this situation, you are stuck with a long call without any way of hedging your risk.

How to make the best of this situation

Every professional trader once in their career has legged into spreads. It is hard to learn your lessons the hard way when you can avoid it.

The best solution is to always enter spreads in the form of a single trade. It is merely an act of foolishness to take an additional risk when you don't need it.

Don't forget multi-leg strategies have multiple commissions and additional risks attached to them and may have certain tax consequences.

Bad situation #5 - Trying to recover your loss by doubling up your investment

No trader likes to lose any trade. Some traders have they're laid down rules such like "I will never sell during the in the money options" or "buy them out of the money options." however, these rules look obvious until they discover the trade is moving against them.

You must understand that Options trading is different from trading stocks.

You must always consider time decay, which is why "double up" isn't something to think about. although leverage is possible when trading options, it can lead to heavy loss.

Therefore, when you find your side in a losing trade, cut the losses, and close the trade to escape any tragedy.

Every trader has been in such a situation, so don't feel left out. When confronted with a situation that goes against their anticipation, most trader breaks their rules and continues trading with the option they started with.

In a situation like this, most traders wished they were right while the market was wrong. Notwithstanding, if you find yourself in such a scenario, what is the next line of action?

How to make the best of this situation

In Options Trading, doubling up your profit to cover your loss is not a strategy that always works. Options are derivatives, meaning that their prices won't move in the same direction or contain the same properties as the underlying asset or stock.

In as much as doubling up can reduce the cost of your pre-contract, it generally increases your risk. When you consider a trade going out of order, and you are anticipating the inconceivable, just step back and reevaluate the situation. Ask the right question like, "If this trade isn't in position, will I make it?" If your answer is negative, then don't think of doing it.

The best option for you is to close the trade, which will surely lead to a loss, and find a better opportunity. Options Trading offer numerous potentials for leverage using moderately low capital; however, if you find yourself going deeper, you can blow your account faster than expected. It is better to accept your current loss and move ahead for better opportunities.

Bad Situation #6 – Neglecting Upcoming Events

The trading market is one that is influenced by the slightest news or event. At times, it is hard to track all events happening in the market.

However, when trading options, you must track dividends and earning dates for your stock.

These two events are crucial to you becoming a successful trader that increases his or her profit.

How to deal with this situation

The only solution is to track upcoming events. There are no two ways about this. Not only is future dividend dates important, but you must also put into consideration past dividend dates. Furthermore, avoid selling options with undecided dividends unless you can handle the risk.

On the other hand, trading options during earning seasons signifies higher volatility with the stock. Are you ready to steer your ship during this period? Well, if you still want to buy options during the earning period, you can choose to sell one option while buying the other.

Bad Situation #7 – Overlooking Index Options

A single stock at times is volatile.

For instance, if there is a key unanticipated news event of a company, it can influence the stock for some times.

Alternatively, even serious havoc in a prominent company, which is among the S&P 500, may not cause the index to swing that much. What does this have to do with Options Trading?

Options Trading based on indexes can moderately protect you from big movements in the market, which is created by singles news of individual stocks.

You can navigate through this situation by minimizing the uncertain influence of market news.

How to get the best of this situation

Consider using strategies that will be profitable when the market remains in credit spreads.

Index movement is less intense and less likely influenced by news compared to other strategies.

Using short spreads is reasonably profitable because the price of the stock remains unchanged.

Short put spreads and short call spreads are neutral to bullish and bearish situation, respectively. Don't forget, spreads involve over one option trade and incur over one commission.

Consider this when making a decision during your trading.

Bad situation #8 – using the out of the money call options

Buying out of the money calls completely is one of the toughest means of making money steadily in Options Trading.

The out of the money call options look attractive for most new traders because they are cheap.

Initially, it looks like the best place to begin. Buying calls looks safer because it matches the pattern most equity traders follow.

All they do is to buy low while selling high. However, if you depend on this strategy, you will steadily lose money as you trade.

So what is the best option?

How to get the best out of this situation

Think about selling out of the money call options on stocks that belong to you like your first strategy.

This is the covered call strategy and important for this situation because it covers your stock position.

This strategy also allows you to get profit on stocks when your stock is bullish but willing to sell it even if the price goes up.

Nevertheless, you have to be cautious because the risk lies in you owning the stock. This risk may be considerable.

While selling the call option may not have any risk on your capital, it surely limits your upside, which further creates risk opportunity.

Bad Situation #9 – Wasting a longer time before using the buyback short strategies

This bad situation boils down to a single piece of advice from certain people who advise traders to be alert always and ready to buy back short strategies timely.

It is quite comfortable to rely on your past success and assume things will continue the way it is when you trade is going the way you anticipated.

Nevertheless, this won't be the situation always because trading working in your favor can suddenly switch to oppose you. Most traders come up with different excuses to wait but don't fall for that trap.

Why do people make this mistake?

- They are expecting to scrape some profit from their trade

- They are expecting the option contract will expire valuelessly

- They don't want to pay any commission

How to get the best out of this situation

If your short options go beyond out of the money and you want to buy it back to remove the risk, don't waste any time, do it.

Here is the general rule in dealing with this situation.

If you can withhold 80% or more of your gain from a particular sale of an option, you should contemplate on buying it back straightaway.

If you don't, a short option may be your undoing when you wait too long.

Keep Learning

No professional will tell you options trading is easy.

It is also intimidating and confusing when you don't understand the basics.

There is every possibility of losing everything you invested, particularly if the trader becomes the trader because he has to fulfill the obligation if the buyer decides to buy the option.

This is just one scenario that an inexperienced trader can term as a scary endeavor.

Nevertheless, you must realize that everything is learnable.

If you can spend adequate time and research about options trading with its various strategies before venturing into, you can be successful.

Even the most experienced and skillful traders attend seminars to upgrade their knowledge because the wealth of information on options trading is vast.

For a trader, you have to find the information, read it, and understand it before implementing it.

Options Trading are very risky; however, you can mitigate the risk involved by deciding correctly.

The only way to decide correctly is by equipping yourself with the necessary knowledge about trading.

"It's not what we do once in a while that shapes our lives. It's what we do consistently."

Anthony Robbins

Chapter Eight

Managing Risk Effectively in Options Trading

If you were to conduct a survey on how risky options trading is, 8 out of 10 would conclude that trading option is risky.

Do you think options trading are risky? It is not an easy question to answer because it depends on you define risk to be.

In as much as risk and reward work together, each person has his own definition of risk.

However, most "trader" describes risk as one of the following. The first group describes it as the probability of earning a profit over the probability of suffering a loss on your investment.

The second group refers to it as the amount of money you lost in comparison to the amount gained during trading. Both sides seem to be absolutely correct. However, I will explore the angle taken by each side.

First Group – Probability of Profit over Probability of Loss

For these traders or investor who regard risk as the probability of their returns over their loss is based on the amount of risk invested.

The risk of their trade is normally on a lesser consideration because there is no expectation of loss.

These traders focus largely on strategies where the likelihood of their profit is higher than their loss.

For instance, the prediction of the trader concerning the underlying asset is correct; using any of the following strategies may be regarded as low risk:

- Deep in the money long put

- Deep in the money long call

- Buy/sell strategy

- A far out of the money naked call

- A far out of the money naked put

Second Group – Amount loss over amount gained

At times, this strategy is called the risk-to-reward ratio. Traders, who use this approach, will get involved in only trades where the gain is much higher to the loss they may incur.

For instance, the trader prediction on the asset is correct; using any of the following strategies is quite a low-risk strategy.

- A lottery ticket

- Out of the money long strangle

- Out of the money long put

- Out of the money long call

Risk and Money Management

To be an effective trader, you must understand the importance of managing your capital and risk exposure. Interestingly, the risk and money management strategy employed here doesn't apply to options trading but to every kind of trading.

Risk is generally unavoidable; however, your exposure to it should not be a key problem. The best strategy for managing your risk effectively is by ensuring you are content with the risk level you take. Besides this, don't expose yourself to risks you can't sustain.

The concept of risk management is also applicable to money management. You shouldn't trade with the amount of capital you can't afford to lose while trading. Therefore, always follow the thumb rule by not overstressing yourself.

Adhering to an effective money and risk management practice is significant to you succeeding in Options trading.

It is a major subject to understand before trading because most people, who overlook this practice, have paid dearly for it. Why should you follow their footstep?

In this chapter, you will understand various methods you can employ in your risk management approach while learning how to control your budget effectively.

Risk Management Techniques

By now, you would have known the importance of risk management as an options trader. It is one of the basic requirement to succeed as a trader because it can create huge problems for you if not properly addressed.

In this section, I will go through the best risk management techniques every active trades must understand to prevent "stories that touch the heart." I hope you understand that statement, especially if you are thinking of investing huge capital. Don't worry; my goal is to help you protect your money by avoiding any risk that is unhealthy for you.

Why use risk management?

Perhaps, you may be wondering why you have to learn about risk management. Well, it is an essential aspect of options trading many people overlook.

Many traders go into the trading market, make some trades, and suddenly, they have made great profits. This is exciting, but with two bad trades, you can blow your account without applying proper risk management. So you see why risk management is an essential ingredient for success in options trading.

Planning your trades – It doesn't matter how many times one has to echo this; you've got to plan your trades. Everything in life requires planning, and with adequate planning, you can come on top of every trade.

Planning will take you to places you never imagine. Before starting any trade, you've got to start from the drawing board. In Options Trading, the difference between failure and loss is planning ahead of time. Two ways of planning ahead of each trading are by using take-profit and stop-loss.

As a trader, you must know the particular price you are willing to buy or sell options. You must consider the profit over the possibility of the stock hitting the anticipated target.

If you can get enough from sure trade, then go for it. However, unsuccessful traders overlook these things even though they may look little. They don't have a plan on what to buy or sell to get a profit. They are like gamblers, gambling with their money and hoping the market will swing to their favor.

These traders may have an unlucky streak of loss, and suddenly their emotions set in. however, emotions have to part to play in Options trading instead of planning and strategizing is the secret. When they make losses, they try to get their money back but continue the same mistake repeatedly. If you plan your trades, you will never be in such a situation and always be on top of the market.

Take Profit and Stop-Loss

We mentioned these two words at the beginning but did you even though what they meant? Did you get to find the meaning through "Google?"

If you are really interested you could have checked the meaning. However, don't worry because all you need is here.

Understanding these terms is a key factor that determines if you will get the sales and profit you want.

A stop-loss is a price at which a trader is willing to sell a stock and collect a loss on that particular trade. This takes place when the trade goes against your anticipation.

The stop-loss will prevent the trade and limit the losses you made. Most traders have the "it will return back" mentality. However, stop-loss helps you to limit that loss.

On the other hand, a take-price is the precise price a trader is willing to sell the stock to take profit from the trade.

It is a situation where the option traded by the trader hits the desired price.

Setting stop-loss points for trades

Sometimes, you have no option but to set stop-loss in order to get profits. However, you can do this by using technical analysis, which requires formulas.

Notwithstanding, you can also use fundamental analysis to complement your decision.

For instance, if an investor decides to hold a stock ahead of earnings as momentum builds, he may decide to sell it before the news gets to the market.

This will hinder more people from investing in the stock while he will make more profit before the stock gets risky.

You can also use the moving averages method. It is a very simple and easy method, which allows you to calculate and track the market.

To do this, you select the amount of a timed average and put it on the stock's chart to determine the time the price reacted.

Furthermore, you will also determine the resistance or support level. Use a trendline to connect the highs and lows that took place within your timed averages.

Ensure you use this for a volatile long-term stock in order to prevent swings in price.

How to calculate your returns

Setting up stop-loss and take-profit can help in calculating your expected return in a trade.

This is important because you can use the rate to measure your profit as an alternative of rationalizing it.

Furthermore, it will help you have an organized way of comparing your trades and sell at the best profitable time.

In addition, you can determine when are the right time to trade and the probability of your profit or loss.

With these risk management techniques, you can prevent things from getting worse.

They are part of your arsenals as a trader if you want to make a profit. Minimizing your risk and increasing your profit should be your priority.

Nine Effective Risk Management Strategy

Getting involved in options trading is a risk you have taken.

A risk that won't be as costly as not employing a risk management strategy for your trades.

You can trade without fear. Yes, it is possible. T

he nine risk management strategies mentioned here have been tested in various situations.

You can make a better investment without losing much (I never promised you a loss-free trading adventure).

You will learn the nine things to watch own when trading and their importance in options trading.

With these nine things, you should be able to obtain a consistent result.

#1 – Allocations Flows downstream

Firstly, you have to go through your asset allocation. Ensure that you diversify all your investments and not put them into single equity.

Some trader put their investment in only places.

This will make your investment weighted on a particular area. however, your goal is to ensure they are not overlapping with each other.

Furthermore, before investment, do research about the company, or else you may end up putting so much where you need to invest a little.

#2 - The significance of Difference

When you diversify your options, this can make the difference you are looking for in an investment. You can use volatile options to protect your overall investments. When it comes to hedging, ETFs are very helpful.

#3 - Watch your risk capital

When trading options, you must look out for your overall risk capital. Don't allow your options to increase beyond 15-20% of your total risk capital. If you decide to exceed this level, you put your investment at risk; additionally, you need to have a plan peradventure the stop-loss is triggered. This may make you lose more than the capital you anticipated.

#4 - Watch option account

You should find out the amount of money in the market if you have an account. On no condition should the money in your account exceed 50% that you decide to put in the market. It is very risky to invest 50% of your money on the market. The best option is to have less than that money in the market.

#5 – Lookout for individualities

Your investment for a single option shouldn't exceed 5% of your capital because if your positions start falling, it won't affect your capital that much. Ensure you don't invest so much on a particular trade.

#6 – Trade only comfortable trades

The challenge with most beginners in trading is that they overlook trades that are comfortable with them. It is hard to understand most of the credit products; however, the bigger issue is that these products are double-leveraged products.

If you are a beginner, you should start with trades you are comfortable with when trading. Ensure you are familiar with the investment because it will save you if you adhere to this risk management strategy.

#7 – Manage your money effectively

Money management is very important in your risk management strategy. Later in this chapter, I will explain more about it. just know that with money management, you use only a part of your money to invest.

This helps you to control your capital and prevent you from losing everything. Money management always goes along with position sizing, which helps you to decide the amount to use for a trade.

Following this strategy, you can determine the amount to invest along with the percentage you are willing to put into any trade.

Some trades can turn haywire, which is why you should invest only a small amount.

With the right money management practice, you can never blow your account, and your risk possibility will always be measured before entering a trade.

#8 – Managing Your Orders

Another effective way of managing your risk is by managing your orders. To do this effectively, you should use place different options order.

Besides using the basic four order types, you can use other options orders to support your risk management strategy.

You should watch out for what will benefit you because it can help in preventing you from selling at an unfavorable price.

You can lock some orders automatically to make a profit while cutting your losses.

By using a limit stop order, you can control when to exit a particular position.

By doing this, you avoid situations where you miss when to take your profit because you are holding the trades' position for a longer time.

#9 – Observe your Options Spreads

Observing your options spreads will give you an idea on the movement of the stock.

For instance, if you buy some calls on a particular stock and sell back at a cheaper out of the money calls, this ends up being a bull call.

It is important to use spread to your advantage by managing your risk. By using spread, you minimize the cost of entering a trade position, limit your overall risk, and reduce the amount to use when trading.

Spreads are helpful for both long and short positions.

You can use spreads to know when to leave the trade and know the trend of the market.

If you are thinking of preventing losses while saving in the long run, you must use options spreads.

Options trading may seem telling a blind man to pass a thread through a needle.

It shouldn't be something complicated, especially if you understand what you need to do.

Limiting your trading risk is non-negotiable if you want to put yourself in a profitable position.

With a good risk management strategy implemented, you can reduce your risk while maximizing your profits when trading.

Ways of Managing Risk

Firstly, we will explore three ways of managing your risk before diving into money management and position sizing.

Risk management using Options Spreads

One of the most important and powerful tools to use in Options trading is options spreads. It is a combination of more than a position on contracts based on the underlying asset in order to produce an overall trading position.

Of course, it won't make sense if you are new to options trading. For instance, if you buy during the "in the money" call on a particular stock and later sell cheaper using the "out of the money" call on the same stock, this amount to creating a spread called "bull call spread."

The call option you decide to use on this trade means that you stand to profit if the stock increases in value; however, it will be a loss if all or some of the money used in buying the stock drops.

Writing calls on the same stock gives you the opportunity to control some part of your initial cost, which helps in reducing the total amount you could have lost.

Every strategy used in options trading requires you using spread, and they are very valuable in managing risk in the market.

Additionally, you can decide to use spread to minimize the upfront costs of moving into a position while reducing the amount of money you may have lost.

With the spread, you theoretically reduce your profit while at the same time minimizing your overall risk.

Managing risk by diversifying

Diversification is an essential risk management strategy most investors used in building their stock portfolio through a hold and buy strategy.

The idea behind this strategy for an investor is that by spreading his investment through various companies and areas creates a balanced portfolio instead of the investors' money being "locked down" in a particular area or company. When you diversify your investment, you are less exposed to risk.

Not many traders consider diversification as an important risk management technique in options trading.

In spite of that, it is still important as you can use it to diversify your trade-in in various ways. While the principle of diversification is the same, it isn't advisable to invest all your capital to a particular investment.

Managing risk through options orders

A comparative way of managing your risk is by using a range of different orders in place. Besides the four primary order types to open and close your trade positions, there are also other ways you can place an order.

Some of these are helpful in your risk management strategy.

For instance, you may file order at the best price available during execution time. The is the ideal way of buying and selling options; however, in a volatile market, you may end up filling an order at a higher or lower price you needed it.

Notwithstanding, if you trigger a limit order, which identifies the minimum and maximum price, you can avoid either selling or buying at an unfavorable price. Besides manually triggering a limit order, some orders can be used automatically to exist a position.

Type of Immediate Risk Management

Now you know about risk management and various strategy to employ, it is time to look at the trend when trading options.

The options market is a changing market, and the market flow in various ways.

Therefore, it is paramount to learn the key terms used when traders talk about market fluctuations.

Delta

Did you know the Greek word for change is Delta? Yes.

In Options trading, it signifies the price change of the underlying security corresponding to the change the price derivative.

At times, many traders refer to it as "hedge ratio."

For instance, the price of an asset rises to $2.8. This means that for each $1 that the stock rises, the call option increases by $2.8.

Normally, the delta increases as the stock get closer to the expiration period of the option. Eventually, the option will reach a delta point of 1.00.

Example for Delta

Let's assume the stock of KNC is valued $3 with a delta of 0.4, and the stock price stood at $48. Peradventure, the stock increases to $49; the value of the stock will increase to $3.4.

However, if it goes the other way round, the value will dip to $2.6. This happens in a similar fashion with any number.

Assuming KNC stock is valued $4.00 with a -0.5 delta with the stock price at $48. If the stock rises rather than the option, the value will fall to $3.50. However, if for some reasons it rises, the value will go up to $4.50.

Gamma

This is an estimation of the total amount the delta changes when there is a price movement of $1.

The Gamma informs you about the "stability" of the delta. A big gamma signifies that the delta can begin to change radically for each small movement.

A long put or long call always yield positive gamma. On the flip side, a short call or short put yield a negative gamma.

 typical graph for both the gamma and delta normally looks like a hill with the top position near the predetermined price. The highest for gamma is at the money options.

With gamma, you can review your position on the profit/loss graph over an extended stock price. If the position is a negative one, then that is risky.

Example of Gamma

For instance, the stock of KNC has a delta value of 0.4 for the call option, whereas it is -0.5 for the option call. If the price of the stock stood at $48 and the gamma is 0.7.

Peradventure, there is a movement, the gamma, and the stock price increase, then the delta will follow suit.

To get the gamma position, you can to compute the position delta change once the price of the stocks moves by a dollar.

Theta

This is a measurement of the rate of change in the theoretical value of an option. It illustrates the time decay, which is an estimation of how w much the option reduces when a day passes by without any volatility of stock movement.

The theta for the put and call option at the same predetermined prices are not equal. The difference between these option lies on the stock cost. The theta for the call is higher when compared to the put when the cost of the stock is positive. However, if the theta call option is lower, the cost will be negative.

Both long puts and long calls always have negative theta, whereas short puts and calls have positive theta. Stocks have zero thetas, which mean it cannot be eroded over time. Because of its extrinsic value, theta is higher at the money options. Theta and gamma are opposite to each other. If theta is positive, then gamma must be negative.

Example of Theta

For instance, the stock of KNC has a price of $4.00, theta value of -0.15, and a stock expiration of 20 days.

The stock put option is valued $4.75 with an expiration period of 80 days with a theta at -0.5.

Assuming the stock price doesn't change after a day, meaning there is no volatility on the option.

Then towards the end of the day, the put reduces to $3.85 while the other stood at $4.70.

From this, the stock with lesser time to expire ends up losing less money than those with larger time.

Vega

This is a valuation on how much the hypothetical value of an option during when the volatility changes by 1 percent.

Volatility is directly proportional to the option price. What this means is that if the volatility is high, the option price will also be high.

Furthermore, the stock price swings if the volatility is high. This creates a possibility for the option to yield result through the expiration.

Because of the changes, that takes place over time, both the long puts and calls have a positive Vega.

Similar to theta, Vega is not influenced by volatility. Therefore, the stock does not have a Vega. If the Vega is positive, it means the position of the options increases as the volatility increases.

Vega can increase if the volatility increase and the higher options are out of the money and in the money. So, a changing option will yield a higher Vega.

Example of Vega

For instance, you have a call option value of $2.00 with a Vega of 0.20 with the stock volatility at 30%.

Peradventure, the volatility increases to 31%, the stock value will increase to $2.20.

Assuming Vega drops to 9% because of some unexplainable situation, the stock value will eventually drop to $1.80.

Money Management and Position Sizing

It is hardly possible to differentiate money and risk management when you are trading options. These two terms are equally important – with money management, you determine the amount of money to use in trading while risk management enables you to control your risk by not losing the money invested.

Therefore, what is the best way of managing your money when trading options? The best strategy most investor use in managing their money is a concept called "Position Sizing." It is deciding the amount of capital to use when entering a particular position when trading.

Nevertheless, to use position sizing effectively, you must consider the amount you want to invest for every single trade in terms of the percentage of your overall capital invested. Position sizing is similar to diversification, but it involves using a small percentage of your overall capital in a single trade.

For instance, you invested 50% of your trading capital to a particular trade, and the trade turned against you, this means you have lost some significant amount of your investment.

However, if you decide to use either 5% or 10% of the capital for each trade and still experience some loss, your capital won't be wiped out.

Improving your money management strategy

Making money shouldn't be anything hard to make if you are trading. It involves the application of certain principles to keeping the profit flowing. Interestingly, some trained monkeys can find winning stock using darts. The issue here is about not giving back your profits in your next trade.

Losing in options trading is inevitable. Having the mentality that you will have a 100% winning rate is unrealistic and unhealthy expectations of having if you are a trader. Losing a trade as a trader is likened to the inventory of a retailer, who has to restock his goals.

Losses to a trader are one of the costs of trading. Once your profit exceeds your costs, you have profitable trading.

There are two ways to profit in the trading market. The first is by taking smaller profits from a large number of traders. This is the method option sellers, high-frequency traders, and market makers make their money. However, the challenge with this model is how to avoid big trade losses that have the potential of wiping out small profits made over time.

The second ways to profit is by making big profits from fewer trades while taking a small loss. Examples of those with this strategy are the black swan traders and the high-growth speculators, whose focus is on targeting the next big crash in the market.

Option sellers focus on strategy, index, and stock. The high-frequency traders find a particular niche and take advantage of the pricing phenomena, whereas the market marker specializes in stocks or securities.

These different traders have the required experience and knowledge to avoid taking big losses while concentrating on a single strategy.

It doesn't matter the kind of approach different traders use, the money management strategy applied is similar.

The general rule for professionals is to never risk above 5% of their total money in their account on a single trade. The secret behind this is that you can easily recover from that risk level.

Even if you had a series of loss, it would take 24 consecutive trade loss to wipe half of your account. In as much as losses in trading are inevitable, having 24 consecutive losses is highly unthinking and an extraordinary stretch that signifies something is wrong with your trading skill and knowledge.

Let me clarify when I say don't rise above 5% of your capital in a single trade. I know some traders will take this the wrong way. Therefore, using several examples, this concept of money management will be clear.

For instance, Greg has a $500k account with his portfolio diversified into five different trades.

Each of these trades has an equal amount of $100k.

Let us assume Greg is conservative in trading and decides to use a 5% loss or spread limit in his trade if he loses 5% of this $500k in his account, that equates to $25k.

When you apply this to all of the $100k investment, that $25k lose signifies you can only lose 25% loss without damaging your overall capital in your account.

The truth is that losses are part of trading, and they are inevitable. However, with proper money management strategy, you will always live to fight the next day.

How to determine position sizing

Understandably, it is not easy to determine the particular size to use when trading, especially if you are a beginner. Nevertheless, there are various means to determine how big your position should be. Furthermore, it is important to note that this is not under the control of your broker but depends on you.

Notwithstanding, you can calculate your position sizing effectively. Before you do that, you need to know about three important things that constitute your position size. These include:

- Account size

- Amount willing to risk

- Stop loss/spread

To calculate the position size, you can use the formula below

Position size = ((Percentage of risk per trade * account size)/spread (stop loss))

How to use position sizing to grow your options trading account

You made a huge trade only to lament that the trading position was small.

On the other hand, you made a loss on a trade, and you are grieving over how big your trading position was.

With the right position sizing, you will surely get high returns.

Doing this, you can move from being a realistic chance taker to a consistently profitable trader that knows his "thing."

However, if this is the opposite of you, how do you deal with this problem that has the potential of wiping your account clean with a single trade?

In this section, you will learn the crucial things to proper position sizing.

Build your trading strategy

It is easier said than done. However, you have to start somewhere, and having a business plan is important. I have already spoken about this in Chapter four of this book.

Give each trade you want to enter a name and have a different strategy for each of them. You should have a trade book to identify your best trade.

Identify your best setups

What are your best trades? You won't know if you don't have taken note of it.

You can decide to take more risk on such trades. However, you have to identify them first before trading.

Develop your second best setup

Perhaps some trades may be below your best setups. These trades are not perfect; you can rate them B.

They are trades that look like a good trade, but you aren't convinced about it, so you nibble.

Well, with some position sizing, you watch the trade get better.

Determine your maximum daily loss

Most traders don't have a loss and profit strategy. However, objective traders, before entering any trade set their loss and profit margins.

If you are a beginner, your maximum loss strategy should be as low as possible.

As time goes on, you can increase your risk level. It is also advisable not to risk above 2% of your capital when trading if you are a beginner. With that risk level, you have something to fall back to when things go haywire.

Think in terms of "percentages"

With your daily maximum loss level established, you can consider each trade in terms of percentage. When you think in terms of percentages, it allows you to scale each trade easily. As you become consistent in your trade, you can increase the amount you want to risk. Remember, consistency is the key.

Don't be rigid

It is understandable that you have to set a risk plan and adhere to it painstakingly. Yes, that is a step towards becoming a professional trader. Never exceed your maximum daily risk level. On no account should you do ever exceed that risk level?

Nevertheless, trading is a fluid activity, which at times you have to amend your plans. Strictly adhering to your risk strategy can make you miss a huge trade. You may be sitting on your rocky chair contemplating the risk involved in the trade while it passes you by.

In addition, you may find yourself in situations where you misjudge the risk on a particular trade only for it to swing against you. Trying to be rigid and perfect can make things go against you.

"You will never find fulfillment trading the markets if you don't learn to appreciate and be satisfied with what you already have."

Yvan Byeajee

Conclusion

There is so much information contained in this book; it contains everything you need to help you begin your journey into options trading. Trading (stock, options, forex, securities, or exchanges) is a process, and every process requires you to practice.

The more you practice, the better you become at it. In the introduction of this book, I clearly stated that success happens when preparation and opportunity meet. I wrote this book with that perspective.

In Chapter 1, we dived into the fundamentals of options trading, whereas, in Chapter 2, I briefly explained how you could manage your options positions.

In Chapter 3, you will learn about the various pricing models in options trading. Additionally, I talked about the importance of knowing how pricing is calculated.

Then Chapter 4 was an enlightening section was you have to learn how to treat options trading like a business. Furthermore, get to know the 10 Ultimate profit secret strategies in Chapter 5. You will learn secret strategies like a straddle, collar call, and strange married put among others.

If you want to know more about the fundamental of the concepts of moneyness, then brush up your knowledge in Chapter 6.

You will also learn the importance of the concept of moneyness. To be a professional, then you must understand the concept of moneyness.

Learning from experience is important because you don't want to make a mistake.

Chapter 7 explores various bad situations professional traders have faced and the best way to deal with such a situation. You don't have to blow your account to learn your lesson.

Finally, get to know how to manage your risk in chapter 7. Losses are inevitable in trading, but if you can minimize your loss and increase your profit, you will be smiling at the end. Get to know more about money management and position sizing.

Yippee! You made it to the end of this informative book "Options Trading – Simplified Beginner's Guide to Make Money with Trading Options in 7 Days."

Undoubtedly, the book is explanatory and mind-blowing because it contains secrets that most professional traders won't tell you.

I have been able to furnish you with every strategy you need to trade like a professional. However, because you were able to cover every topic, does not mean you know everything.

You have to expand your horizons to know more. This is where you will find the perfection you want.

"Trading effectively is about assessing probabilities, not certainties."
Yvan Byeajee

Glossary

Asks Price – The price will cost an investor to buy an option. Also the best price available from a seller. The offer price of an option.

At the Money – A put option is a situation where the predetermined price is the same as the current underlying asset price

Bear Call Spread – An option strategy that uses calls, which can be used when an investor expects the underlying stock, will drop in price

Bearish – A situation where you expect the price of an option or asset to drop in price

Bid Price – The price at which an option is sold

Binomial Options Pricing Model – Abbreviated as BOPM; the trio Cox, Ross, and Rubinstein develop this pricing model in 1979

Black Scholes Options Pricing Model – A pricing model based on various factors, including the price of the underlying stock, the predetermined price, expiration date, and volatility.

Bear Put Spread – A strategy that allows investors simultaneously buying at a higher predetermined price while selling at a lower predetermined price on the same asset with the same expiry date.

Broker – A company or individual that executes orders for a client to either buy or sell financial instruments

Bull Market – When the trend of the market is moving upward

Bullish – A market situation where one anticipates a rise in the price of the financial instrument

Call option – An option that gives the buyer the right to purchase 100 shares of the stock at the predetermined price for each share before the expiration of the contract. A call option gives the buyer the right to purchase the underlying shares at a predetermined price, on or before the predetermined date

Covered Call – A strategy that allows an investor to make returns from existing stock when they are neutral

Dividend – Payment made by a company to its shareholders. It is a representation of their shares of profits

Expiry or **Expiration Date** – The day at which an option contract expires or ceases to exist

Extrinsic value – A representation of the amount someone is willing to pay in anticipation that the market will favor him or her within the period of the option. Extrinsic value is also the portion of an option price, which exceeds its intrinsic value.

Financial instrument – A virtual or real asset, which has an inherent monetary value. Examples include currencies, options, shares, stocks, commodities, futures, etc.

Hedging – an investment strategy that allows investors to minimize their risk of holding a particular investment

Holder – The buyer of an option

Implied Volatility – An estimation of the underlying security or asset future volatility as forecasted by the current market price of the option

In the Money - A call option in the money situation occurs when the stock price is higher than the predetermined price whereas the put option occurs in a situation where the stock price is lower than the predetermined price

Intrinsic Value - The difference between the stock price and the predetermined price. The Intrinsic value also refers to the in the money portion of a put or call contract current market price

Leg – The combination of different trading positions

Limit Order – An order type used to sell or buy an option at a definite minimum or maximum price respectively

Liquidity – A measurement at which a particular financial instrument can be sold or bought at ease without influencing the price of the stock

Long Call – A strategy use when the expectation of the underlying asset or stock is bullish

Long Option –

Long Position – A position where the investor is anticipating a rise in the price of the stock

Long Put – Opposite of long call; occurs when the underlying asset is bearish

Margin – This has different meaning depending on the context when used. In options trading, it is the amount of cash you must hold in a trading account when selling a contract

Married Put – An option strategy, which uses options and stocks

Model – see Pricing Model

Moneyness – Refers to the predetermined price as it relates to the current price of the stock (underlying asset)

Neutral Market – A situation where the entire market is comparatively stable; meaning it is either bearish or bullish

Option Contract – the right to sell or buy an asset at a predetermined price within a specified timeframe

Option Pricing Model - A mathematical models, which uses certain variables to estimate the theoretical price of an option. The theoretical price is an estimation of what an option is worth after using every recognizable input

Options Trader – An individual who buys or sells option contracts

Options Trading – The art of buying and selling options contracts

Out of the money – A situation in options trading when the option does not have intrinsic value. What this means is that the call option is out-of-the-money when the predetermined price is higher than the stock price

Premium – The price received or paid for an option in the market.

Put Option – A situation where the holder has the right to sell the stock or asset at a predetermined price in the future. The put option is similar to when you have a "short on a stock."

Risk – The potential of losing a particular trade

Roll – A transaction in options trading that requires closing one position while opening another one for the same underlying stock.

Spread – An option position triggered by buying one option while selling another option using the same underlying asset or security

Stock Option – An option where the main asset is stock

Strategy – A preconceived logical plan including a follow-up action to that position

Strike Price – Also known as a predetermined price

Technical Analysis – A type of analysis that enables you to predict the future price movement of stock by observing the historical stock price movement

Time Decay – Same as expiration date

Time Value – Same as extrinsic value

Trade Size – The total number of contracts or shares used for a trading position

Trading Style – An approach a trader takes to follow to trade

Trend - A continuous movement in a trading market

Underlying Security – Same as Underlying stock

Underlying Stock/Asset – The stock at which a particular option's value is dependent and changes hands once the option is assigned or exercised

Value -

Volatility – the up and down movement of a stock price

Volume - The total number of stock shares or option contracts traded during a given period.

Write—To sell an option. A writer is an investor that sells options

www.ingramcontent.com/pod-product-compliance
Lightning Source LLC
Chambersburg PA
CBHW071353210526
45465CB00001B/80